Teaching in the Global Business Classroom

Teaching in the Global Business Classroom

Carol Dalglish

Associate Professor, Brisbane Graduate School of Business, Queensland University of Technology, Australia

Peter Evans

Principal, Leadership Education Australia

Edward Elgar

Cheltenham, UK • Northampton, MA, USA

Published by
Edward Elgar Publishing Limited
The Lypiatts
15 Lansdown Road
Cheltenham
Glos GL50 2JA
UK

Edward Elgar Publishing, Inc.
William Pratt House
9 Dewey Court
Northampton
Massachusetts 01060
USA

A catalogue record for this book
is available from the British Library

Library of Congress Control Number: 2008927969

ISBN 978 1 84720 055 6 (cased)

Printed and bound in Great Britain by MPG Books Ltd, Bodmin, Cornwall

Contents

PART I

1. Introduction to international business education

> You learn from foreigners that there is more than one path to a goal. Effective wealth creation demands that we use all the paths available to us. (Hampden-Turner and Trompenaars 1993: 16, cited in Sinclair and Wilson 1999: 27)

International education around the world has grown exponentially in recent years. Tertiary education around the world is becoming 'internationalized': that is, there is an increasing mix of domestic and international students in classes. Many Western countries including the United States, the United Kingdom, Australia, New Zealand, Canada and South Africa provide education for significant numbers of foreign students from an increasingly diverse range of countries. 'Foreign' education is big business. Initially these students came from the region in which the university operated, that is, there was extensive movement between European countries, Britain attracted students from the Commonwealth where there were historical links, South Africa attracted students from other parts of Africa, and Australia and New Zealand's biggest source countries were in South East Asia.

As of 2007, the following are currently the top source countries for international students:

- USA: the top five source countries are India, China, South Korea, Japan and Canada. These five countries make up 46 per cent of the foreign students studying in higher education in the States.
- UK: the top five non-EU source countries are China, the USA, India, Malaysia and Hong Kong. These students make up 49 per cent of the non-EU foreign students.
- Australia: the top five source countries, that make up 56 per cent of the total foreign students include China, India, Malaysia, Hong Kong and Indonesia.
- Canada: the top five source countries make up 46 per cent of foreign students studying in Canada and include China, the USA, France, India and South Korea.
- New Zealand: the top five source countries make up 80 per cent of foreign student numbers in New Zealand and include China, South

Korea, Japan, the USA and India. (http://aei.gov.au/AEI/Publications
AndResearch.)

As can be seen from the above figures, despite the overall diversity of countries whose citizens travel to study, these five primary English language destinations are drawing from the same source countries, in particular, China
and India. Even without considering the wide range of countries that make
up the other '50 per cent', the diversity of culture, education system and
worldview apparent within these primary source countries is considerable.

About 1.6 million students study outside their home country and of
those over 500 000 study in the US (Mazzarol and Hosie, cited in Avirutha
et al. 2005). Education is the third-largest export in Australia (Marginson
2002) with over 100 000 foreign students studying at Australian universities
in 2000, and it is predicted that this will rise to over 500 000 by the year 2022
(IDP 2002).

AEI (2006) provides the total numbers of international students for the
main English-speaking provider countries:

- USA (2004) 572 509.
- UK (2004) 325 760 (214 190 non-EU).
- Australia (2004) 151 799.
- Canada (2004) 70 035.
- New Zealand (2004) 50 213. (http://aei.gov.au/AEI/Publications
  AndResearch.)

One of the primary advantages of studying abroad is to learn a new
culture and adapt to a new learning environment which offers real-life experiences (Avirutha et al. 2005). This is particularly important in business
education where graduates will eventually work across a range of countries
and cultures. Cross-cultural understanding has an important impact on
business effectiveness in an increasingly global environment, and what is
taught in the classroom needs to be relevant to all the students wherever
geographically they follow their careers.

Despite this, and the fact that Australia, the US, the United Kingdom
and many of the other host countries of international students are themselves extremely culturally diverse communities, business education
remains essentially monocultural in form and Anglo-American in content
(De Cieri and Olekalns 2001). The teaching and learning implications of
such a large, very diverse international student population have yet to be
addressed at most institutions of higher education. Not only are there an
increasing number of international students on business programmes
around the world, but they are coming from an increasingly diverse range

of countries as can be seen above. For many of these students, their first language is other than English, though business classes, particularly at MBA and postgraduate levels, are traditionally taught in English. Their experience of tertiary education is often significantly different from that which they encounter at the 'Western' institutions. Their experiences are also different from each other. This raises challenges for teachers who are faced with sizeable classes made up of a combination of domestic and diverse international students.

These international students may want to understand the 'Western' way of doing things, but may not be familiar or comfortable with the processes used to facilitate learning (Pincas 2001). Business classrooms traditionally use a range of Western teaching and learning strategies that focus on critical analysis, oral discussion, problem solving and the possibility of multiple solutions using case studies and discussion groups that require active participation by the students, which many international students find unfamiliar. Every student comes to the classroom with a set of behaviours and characteristics that makes him or her unique (Ryan 2000; Jones 2005). But international students also come with their own expectations arising from the educational practices of their home communities. Their potential lack of participation in classroom activities puts constraints on classroom interaction and learning. It also means that nothing that they have to teach about their way of doing things, is learned.

Tertiary institutions have much vested in the successful education of all their students, including their increasing numbers of international students. Many tertiary institutions have become financially dependent on the substantial fee income from international students. As more and more institutions in more countries begin to compete for this lucrative student body, so recruitment by demonstrating quality and relevance becomes an increasing challenge. Around the world business schools are competing for accreditation as evidence of their quality. These accrediting bodies are concerned about the learning experience of all the students, and in the case of EQUIS (European Quality Improvement System of the European Foundation for Management Education (EFMD)) accreditation, the international nature of the students, staff and programme are essential to success:

> Institutions that are accredited by EQUIS must demonstrate not only high levels of quality in all dimensions of their activities, but also a high degree of internationalisation. With companies recruiting worldwide, with students going to get their education outside their home countries, and with schools building alliances across borders and continents, there is a rapidly growing need to be able to identify those institutions in other countries that deliver high standards of education in international management. (www.efmd.org/html/Accreditations)

Ranking of business schools and programmes is also on the increase and most use graduate feedback as an element. Not feedback from home-grown students only, but from all graduates. The learning experience of international students therefore becomes of critical importance – and all business students are seeking for their programmes to be relevant to their future career needs. This raises a range of challenges which move beyond the concerns of effective teaching and learning to institutional survival and success. It also means that effective teaching and learning and the role of those who facilitate learning are in the front line.

THE INTERCULTURAL CLASSROOM

The potential benefits of this student diversity are many (Cox and Blake 1991). Not only do international students bring significant revenue to the university but they also provide an opportunity for intercultural learning, for a sharing of knowledge and perspectives that could be so important for success in today's global business environment (Harding 2004). Yet research suggests that cultural engagement is largely unidirectional – Australian (US and UK) students expect international students to adjust to them, not vice versa (cited in Marginson 2002). In classrooms with students from Europe, North and South America, Asia, India, Africa and Australia, the potential for intercultural understanding and skills development is enormous. But it will not happen without assistance. Many international students spend most of their time with other students who speak their language or who come from a similar cultural background. The host communities are not different in this respect. Therefore many international students, who come to study in a foreign country, learn about local business practices in the classroom but gain no practical experience of what local businesses, or local people, are like.

The attitudes and skills of teachers are of critical importance to the internationalization of the classroom (Anderson 2001). Their attitudes impact on providing effective learning experiences to all students in culturally diverse classrooms.

A number of questions then arise: what do the facilitators of learning, the teachers, lecturers and tutors, expect? What do they see as the benefits or disadvantages of this international diversity in their classrooms? What do they need to know and do to be effective in the classrooms of the twenty-first century?

Many tertiary institutions include 'internationalization' as one of their objectives. But it is often unclear what that means. International student recruitment forms one aspect of internationalization, but will not necessarily increase the internationalization of the institution as many international students share little about their countries and live together with fellow nationals, so learn little about the country in which they study. The concept of 'Internationalization at home supports the view that much about internationalization can be taught at home' (Coyne 2003; Sandstrom 2003) but this requires the acknowledgement that internationalism requires a further examination of the learning environment, the curriculum, and the attitudes and abilities of teachers.

Attitudes to international students are varied. Many teachers see them simply as a source of revenue, believing that institutions are attracting international students as a means of enhancing the 'bottom line'. These teachers may adopt a strategy of exclusion – of denying that there is an issue. The difference remains invisible. The additional challenges brought about by international student concerns about being 'invisible' (after all they are paying a lot of money to be ignored) can also cause resentment among teachers as student–teacher ratios grow.

Others see that as students have chosen to study within these institutions, they must expect to be treated in the same way as all other students. No adjustment need be made either to their learning style or approach to business practice as they meet the general entry requirements. Many local students endorse and pressure teachers to adopt this approach. This leads to assimilation strategies–demanding homogeneity.

Many teachers recognize that if international students are to learn effectively, strategies need to be adopted that acknowledge their different backgrounds and learning experiences. This may lead to an integration approach, where students are helped to develop what are considered relevant competencies, attitudes and behaviours. This requires additional work on someone's part – either the teacher, or support services – which may be viewed as 'unfair' to domestic students, and more work for the teacher. However positive, it is still a deficit model, an assumption that students whose first language is not English, or who lack specific cultural knowledge, are in some way 'inferior' despite the fact that they may speak several languages, have travelled widely and be academically well qualified. This ethnocentric view of the world is now daily being challenged as we become aware that there are many different ways of being successful, and that often the key is to understand the 'rules' in any given context.

Very few teachers appear to have considered that international students are a resource that will enable all students to learn how to operate in a multicultural world (Dalglish 2006). The mutual adaptation model (Roosevelt 1996; Ballard and Clanchy 1997; Dalglish 2006) where difference is acknowledged and the difference forms the basis of mutual understanding – rather than a move to change to one particular perspective – is rarely implemented.

These four possible attitudes provide a model for understanding attitudes to international students. They reflect attitudes to those who are culturally and linguistically different. The particular view held by the lecturer or facilitator of learning is critical to internationalizing the curriculum as each person will be structuring the teaching and learning process based on a particular belief set (Cunningham 2005).

THE PURPOSE OF THIS BOOK

Few lecturers have been taught how to address the issues raised by the complex multicultural classroom (Cunningham 2005), whatever their personal perspective. That is the purpose of this book: to enhance teachers' understanding of the issues to be addressed in the global classroom and to provide practical strategies that will enhance the learning of all students, wherever they come from, and assist the teachers to overcome their frustrations with such a complex work environment and gain greater satisfaction from their classroom experiences.

Most teachers care about their students' learning, wherever those students may come from. They often have a passion for their discipline and want to communicate their enthusiasm to their students. Cultural diversity complicates this process, but it is possible to change this apparently insurmountable challenge to an opportunity for a more rewarding teaching and learning experience for all concerned.

STRUCTURE OF THE BOOK

The book is divided into two parts – the first part explores the 'what' and the 'why' of teaching in the global business classroom, and consists of five chapters addressing such issues as understanding intercultural education, culture shock, learning and cross-cultural communication. The second part addresses the 'how'. It provides practical guidance for teachers in the primary areas of concern in university business education: curriculum design, lecturing, classroom participation, working in groups, using case studies, assessment and distance learning.

REFERENCES

aei.gov.au/AEI/PublicationsAndResearch, 'International student numbers', accessed July 2006.

Anderson, Mary (2001), 'Cross-cultural communication in the global classroom: issues and implications', Melbourne: Monash University.

Avirutha, Anupong, Mai X. Bui, Geraldine H. Goodstone, Kenya Reid, et al. (2005), 'Current overview and future of business higher education', *Futurics*, **29** (1/2).

Ballard, Brigid and John Clanchy (1997), *Teaching International Students*, Sydney: IDP Education Australia.

Coyne, David (2003), 'Internationalisation at home and the changing landscape', Internationalisation at Home Conference, Malmo University, April.

Cox, Taylor H. and Stacy Blake (1991), 'Managing cultural diversity: implications for organisational competitiveness', *Academy of Management Executive*, **5** (3).

Cunningham, Donna J. (2005), 'Teaching multiculturalism in an age of terrorism: a business perspective', *Cross Cultural Management*, **12** (2).

Dalglish, C. (2006), 'The international classroom: challenges and strategies in a large business faculty', *International Learning Journal*, **12** (6): 85–94.

De Cieri, Helen and Mara Olekalns (2001), 'Workforce diversity in Australia: challenges and strategies for diversity management', Melbourne: Monash University.

Hampden-Turner, C. and A. Trompenaars (1993), *The Seven Cultures of Capitalism*, New York: Doubleday.

Harding, S. (2004), *International at QUT*, Brisbane: QUT, June.

IDP Education Australia (2002), *Global Student Mobility*, Sydney: IDP.

Jones, Lisa A. (2005), 'The cultural identity of students: what teachers should know', *Kappa Delta Pi Record*, **41** (4).

Marginson, Simon (2002), 'The phenomenal rise of international degrees down under', *Change*, **34** (3): 34–43.

Nahal, Anita (2005), 'Cultural collisions', *Diverse Issues in Higher Education*, **22** (20).

Pincas, Anita (2001), 'Culture, cognition and communication in global education', *Distance Education*, **22** (1): 30–51.

Roosevelt, Thomas R. Jnr (1996), *Redefining Diversity*, New York: American Management Association.

Ryan, Janette (2000), *A Guide to Teaching International Students*, Oxford: OCSLD.

Sandstrom, Shirin (2003), 'Networking for internationalisation at home in nursing education', Internationalisation at Home Conference, Malmo University, April.

Sinclair, Amanda and Valerie Britton Wilson (1999), *The Culture-Inclusive Classroom*, Melbourne: Melbourne Business School, University of Melbourne.

www.efmd.org/html/Accreditations, accessed July 2006.

2. The challenges of the international, multicultural business classroom

> The idea of a corporate global village where a common culture unifies the practices of business around the world is more dream than reality. (Rosabeth Moss Canter, cited in Schneider and Barsoux 1997)

ISSUES RAISED BY THE PRESENCE OF INTERNATIONAL STUDENTS

One of the primary advantages for students of studying abroad is to learn a new culture and adapt to a new learning environment with real-life experiences (Avirutha et al. 2005). International students also provide benefit to local students who may not be aware of international differences. This is particularly important in business education where graduates will eventually work across a range of countries and cultures. Cross-cultural understanding has an important impact on business effectiveness in an increasingly global environment, and what is taught in the classroom needs to be relevant to all the students wherever geographically they follow their careers.

Students choose particular institutions because they believe that the curriculum and teaching and learning practices will assist them to get employment. They are looking for content knowledge that reflects the demands of the workplace and processes that equip them to transfer their learning to their employment. They are also looking for a 'campus' experience which is increasingly difficult to provide with so many students having to work part-time to support their studies. This has a range of implications for how internationalization is conceptualized and how an institution meets student learning needs (Dalglish 2005).

An opportunity for intercultural learning, for a sharing of knowledge and perspectives that could be so important for success in today's global business environment, exists within these global classrooms (Harding 2004). Yet research suggests that intercultural engagement is not common. In classrooms with students from Europe, North and South America, Asia, India, Africa and Australia, the potential for intercultural understanding and skills development is enormous. But it will not happen without assistance and this raises a number of issues that need to be addressed (Pincas 2001). One of the assumptions of this book is that the ideal is a classroom that provides an effective learning environment for everyone.

The issues identified by staff and students include a range of both personal and educational issues. These personal issues are relevant as they may well impact on the student's ability to concentrate and understand the importance of what is being learnt (Ballard and Clanchy 1997; Sinclair and Britton Wilson 1999; Ryan 2000; Dalglish 2005).

Personal issues, created by the fact that students are away from familiar environments, such as homesickness, culture shock and associated grief and stress created by family expectations, can impair a student's ability to participate. Culture shock has a chapter of its own to explain what it is and why it has such a strong impact.

Language issues are very diverse and include many different aspects such as inadequate English language ability, particularly in listening and speaking; and the broad range of discipline-specific language and concepts that are often difficult to grasp and are not likely to have been learned in general language programmes. Contextual issues are important, and numerous assumptions are made about students' contextual understanding. In-depth understanding of the local culture and norms is often taken for granted. There is also a risk that lack of awareness that different words mean different things in different national contexts may mean the teacher and the students understand what is being said, but their understanding is significantly different from each other's. Without discussion this 'misunderstanding' may not become apparent.

Different participation practices: international students are often very quiet, appear not to listen to or understand instructions, and need to be checked individually. It is perceived that they require a lot more time than domestic students. It can appear that they come to pass exams rather than learn. International students also appear to want face-to-face contact with lecturers rather than electronic or telephone contact, and this is very time-consuming. It is perhaps useful to reflect on how you would respond if you were in a class where everyone was different in some significant way from you, and you were listening and learning in a second language.

Expectations: there appears to be a lack of shared expectations as to what will occur in the class, what the teaching and learning experience will involve. Different cultures have every different perspectives on learning. In many European and Asian classrooms students are not expected to engage personally with the lecturer but to absorb what is provided. Students come with the learning expertise that they have developed as a result of their previous learning experience, which may be very different from the one they encounter in a foreign country.

Previous experiences of learning for many international students lead them not to challenge the information they are given. They seek the right answer. They are trained as the recipients of learning rather than active learners. Often there is the expectation that the teacher will know the right answer and all they have to do is learn from it. They will accept the teacher's truth. This is most apparent amongst students from Asian countries, but they are not the only students who exhibit dependent behaviour. Many students appear to be unfamiliar with the expectations of critical analysis, oral presentations, participation and debate.

Many cultures have a high level of respect for teachers. As a result they will not challenge. Even to ask questions can suggest that the lecturer is not being effective:

> If a lecturer does not answer a student's question in class but asks the other students what they think, in my country we would think that the teacher is either poorly qualified or lazy. But in Australia this way of not giving the answer . . . it is common in our class, even when the Professor is our teacher. (Third-year Thai student) (Ballard and Clanchy 1997: 1)

> The other students ask many questions and even argue with the professor. I could never do that, because I do not think that is right behaviour. I do not want to become like Australian students. (Second-year Thai undergraduate) (Ballard and Clanchy 1997: 15)

It is also apparent that in some cultures the achievements of the students are seen to be a shared responsibility between students and teachers. The idea, prevalent in the 'West', that learning is entirely the responsibility of the student, that there is no personal relationship between teacher and student, is not always clearly understood in other countries. In Taiwan for example, students expressed their desire for achievement by stating that they would be the best students I (the teacher) had ever had. They clearly saw a relationship between their achievement and my status as a teacher.

Support issues are important. There is a need for students to support each other to reduce isolation. There is also a need for institutional support for students, both academically and socially. It is important that lecturers have access to information outlining what support services are available for international students.

Professional development issues: lecturers need better education and training with regard to international students. This is essential if the institution is to deliver what it promises and lecturers are to fulfil their functions in a way that gives satisfaction to both the students and themselves.

Group work: the integration of domestic with international students in groups is often difficult because of language difficulties, preconceived views and time pressures. The difficulties with tutorials and group work require lecturing and tutorial staff to have patience, firmness and understanding.

Teaching challenges: lack of contextual knowledge can be a problem in both teaching and assessment, as it can make understanding more difficult. Students may need longer for examinations. The presence of international students is seen to curb the amount of material that can be covered, and the amount of participation and discussion that occurs. It can lead to the teacher being less specific in trying to globalize the issues. More repetition and explanation appears to be required and there is a need to be careful with choice of words. It is often difficult to know at what level to pitch the class, and this can lead to a tendency to teach to the lowest level of domestic students (without consideration of the actual level of international students). International students often appear to be passive learners and there is a need to choose learning resources and activities carefully and consider different types of assessment. In many cases these are perceptions rather than fact, but in the classroom as elsewhere, perceptions are reality.

So how do we deal with these apparent cultural differences? Why do students from different cultural backgrounds react so differently to the 'Western' classroom culture? The next section will look at some of the dimensions of culture to develop an understanding of the different assumptions that underlie the different ways in which people from different cultures interpret the world. Each national culture is different, with significant variance within each nation. It is not possible for a lecturer to understand all the possible variations that might exist in any class, and nor is it necessary. However there are some underlying themes that can be incorporated into teaching practice that will support the different approaches to teaching and learning that emanate from different parts of the world.

THE MEANING OF CULTURE AND ITS IMPACT

> A fish only discovers its need for water when it is no longer in it. Our own culture is like water to a fish. It sustain us. We live and breathe through it. (Trompenaars and Hampden-Turner 2002: 20)

We take culture so much for granted that defining it is difficult. Management scholar Ed Schein (1985) defined culture as: 'a set of basic assumptions – shared solutions to universal problems of external adaptation (how to survive) and internal integration (how to stay together) – which have evolved over time and are handed down from one generation to another'.

There are a number of layers of culture. The outer layer – the explicit products of the cultural or the artifact level – includes the observable reality of a culture such as language, food, buildings, fashions and art. These are symbols of a deeper level of culture. The middle layer includes the norms and values. Norms are the mutual sense a group has of what is right and wrong; values are the shared sense of what ought to be, as distinct from what is. At the core of culture is the basic underlying set of assumptions (Schein 1985; Hampden-Turner and Trompenaars 1993). When you question these basic assumptions you are often asking questions that have not been asked before. The assumptions are taken for granted and assumed to be immutable. For example, in countries such as the Netherlands, Norway or Australia you may cause irritation if you ask why people are equal – a basic assumption of those cultures.

Despite the growing similarities at the artifact level of culture, as communication and travel suggest that the world is getting smaller and therefore we are becoming more alike, this is misleading. The advent of the European Union has not reduced the differences between the French, Irish and Germans. The collapse of the Soviet Union has led to extraordinary displays of national and ethnic differences. The regional tensions showed themselves most dramatically in the former Yugoslavia. It seems almost as though the pressure for integration, the process of globalization, is in fact creating an equal, if not stronger pressure for divergence as a statement of difference, as a reflection of the deeper levels of culture (Kluckholn and Strodtbeck 1961; Triandis 1972).

One way to understand how national cultures differ is to examine their values. Geert Hofstede (1980, 1999) identified five value dimensions in research spanning 18 years, involving more than 160 000 people from more than 60 countries. This research identified five dimensions: individualism versus collectivism, power distance, uncertainty avoidance, masculinity versus feminity, and long-term time orientation versus short-term time orientation. The qualitative research of Arvind V. Phatak (1983) identified two other dimensions: formality versus informality, and causal versus urgent attitudes to time. Each culture has its own combination of these attitudes and values that determine what is right and wrong and what the fundamentals of survival are.

Each student and teacher brings to the learning situation the values and attitudes of their culture. Many of these core values are assumed to be shared by others because they are the fundamentals of the way life is – they have seldom been talked about, let alone discussed or challenged. It is often these unacknowledged assumptions that create miscommunication and impair learning in the global business classroom.

The values embedded in a culture influence the behaviour of teachers and students, as well as their reaction to each other and the learning environment. As Hofstede (1999) explains, relationships between people in a society are affected by the values programmed in the minds of these people. Because teaching and learning is heavily dependent on interpersonal relationships, recognition of these different values is crucial to providing an appropriate learning environment for people from diverse cultures.

Trompenaars and Hampden-Turner (2002), drawing on the work of Parson (1951), provide a framework of five dimensions of culture which impact on the nature of the student–teacher relationship.

Universalism versus Particularism (Rules versus Relationships)

The universalist approach is that what is good and right can be defined and always applies. In a particularist culture greater attention is paid to obligations and relationships and less to abstract rules.

In the classroom the universalist will focus more on rules than relationships, will clearly define mutual obligation and insist that these obligations are complied with. An example might be that there are clear guidelines about the penalty for late submission of work. This penalty is laid out very specifically and applied to everyone who submits late. In the classroom the particularist will focus more on relationships than on rules. The rules are easily changed in response to the changing nature of circumstances for each individual.

Communitarianism versus Individualism (the Group versus the Individual)

With the individualist approach it is more important to focus on individuals so that they can contribute to the community as and if they wish. The communitarian perspective considers the community first. Individualistic cultures make frequent use of the 'I' form. People achieve alone and assume personal responsibility. People prefer to undertake activities in pairs or on their own. In communitarian cultures the use of 'We' is more frequent. People ideally achieve in groups and assume joint responsibility. In the learning context the teacher and the learner are equally responsible for the student's success.

Neutral versus Emotional (the Range of Feelings Expressed)

Should the nature of our interactions in the classroom be objective and detached, or is expressing emotion acceptable? In neutral cultures relationships in class are generally instrumental, and about achieving objectives. In more emotional cultures, the expression of emotion is acceptable. In the classroom neutral cultures express themselves by behaving in a cool self-possessed manner with personal feelings seen to be inappropriate. In more culturally emotional contexts thoughts and feelings are revealed verbally and non-verbally. Touching, gesturing and strong facial expressions are common.

Diffuse versus Specific (the Range of Involvement)

When the whole person is involved in the teaching–learning relationship there is real, personal contact, instead of the relationship being determined by the specifics of the role. In many cultures diffuse relationships are not only preferred but necessary, and there is an assumption of a holistic relationship between teacher and students that extends beyond the delivery of subject expertise. In a culture that values specificity, principles and consistent moral standards are independent of the person being addressed. The relationship is specific and purposeful. In diffuse cultures morality is situational depending on the person and context encountered – rules are not drawn up as to the specific nature of the relationship. So acceptance of extenuating circumstances is accepted as the norm.

Achievement versus Ascription (how Status is Accorded)

Achievement means that you are judged on what you have achieved. Ascription means that status is attributed to you as the result of birth, age, educational level, connections and so on. In the achievement-oriented classroom the use of titles is only used when relevant to task. Respect for the teacher is based on how effective he or she is. In ascription-oriented cultures there is extensive use of titles to clarify status. Respect for the teacher is seen as a measure of the students' commitment to learning and the university they are attending.

Implications

Wherever we as teachers sit within these cultural frameworks, all our students will not share our assumptions. The extent to which we modify our behaviour will be a personal decision, but it is important that there is acknowledgement and understanding that the students are behaving in accordance with well-developed cultural norms; to behave differently they will need to understand what is expected, how to behave and why it is necessary for them to change.

A MODEL FOR EFFECTIVE LEARNING

To assist the process of internationalization and improve the student learning experience to enable students to operate effectively in an international multicultural business environment, a conceptual model has been developed to reflect the different elements of the learning experience. The nature of the student learning experience is dependent on the student, the design, delivery and assessment of the curriculum, and the pedagogy and attitudes of teachers in a complex relationship (Figure 2.1).

The literature and feedback from student focus groups (Dalglish 2002; Jones 2005; Nahal 2005) enhances our understanding of what needs to be addressed in each of the elements of the student learning experience.

All three of the elements – students, curriculum and teachers – have an impact on the student learning experience. It is necessary therefore to address all three of the elements in order to have a positive impact on student learning, with each activity building on and enhancing the others.

Learning support will enable international students to focus on their areas of need (different pedagogy, epistemological understanding,

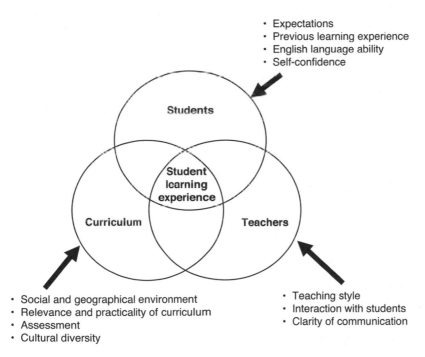

- Expectations
- Previous learning experience
- English language ability
- Self-confidence

Students

Student learning experience

Curriculum

Teachers

- Social and geographical environment
- Relevance and practicality of curriculum
- Assessment
- Cultural diversity

- Teaching style
- Interaction with students
- Clarity of communication

Figure 2.1   The learning environment

language and so on) and help them make the transition from previous learning models and expectations to the philosophy and methods used in the new classroom.

An examination of the curriculum will help define what is meant by 'internationalization' of the curriculum – be it content, context or pedagogy.

Providing a genuinely international context to learning for all students will enable them to place their learning in the context of international business and be aware of the impact of globalization and cross-cultural issues on business practices.

Teachers are the key to facilitating the student learning experience, and enabling teachers to be more effective in the classroom with students from diverse international backgrounds in areas of design, management and assessment, as well as enhancing their ability to engage more effectively with students from multiple backgrounds, will have a positive impact on student learning. It will also provide a more rewarding professional environment for teachers.

It is vital that institutions are clear about the nature of the learning experience that they are offering students. Not just the content, but the learning processes, the social activities and the links to potential employment. International students are looking at the world from a different perspective, assessing the relevance and quality of their course of study to fit into a context often quite different from the country in which they are studying. To be successful, not only in generating income but also in equipping students for their future careers, universities need to listen to students, prospective students and those on the ground in countries around the world to ensure that what is offered continues to meet emerging needs.

REFERENCES

Anderson, Mary (2001), 'Cross-cultural communication in the global classroom: issues and implications', Melbourne: Monash University.

Anderson, M. and D. Moore (1998), 'Classroom Globalisation: an investigation of teaching methods to address the phenomenon of students from multiple national cultures in business school classrooms', working paper, Monash University, Melbourne.

Avirutha, Anupong, Mai X. Bui, Geraldine H. Goodstone and Kenya Reid (2005), 'Current overview and future of business higher education', *Futurics*, **29**(1/2).

Ballard, Brigid and John Clanchy (1997), *Teaching International Students*, Sydney: IDP Education Australia.

Dalglish, C. (2002), 'Promoting effective learning in a multicultural classroom', EDINEB Conference, Guadalahar, Mexico.

Dalglish, C. (2005), 'Expectations and reality – international student reflections on studying in Australia, paper presented at AIEC Conference, Gold Coast.

Hampden-Turner, C. and A. Trompenaars (1993), *The Seven Cultures of Capitalism*, New York: Doubleday.

Harding, S. (2004), *International at QUT*, Brisbane: QUT report, June.

Hofstede, G. (1980), *Culture's Consequences: International Differences in Work Related Values*, Beverly Hills, CA: Sage.

Hofstede, G. (1999), 'The universal and specific in 21st century global management', *Organizational Dynamics*, Summer: 39–41.

Jones, Lisa A. (2005), 'The cultural identity of students: what teachers should know', *Kappa Delta Pi Record*, **41**(4).

Kluckholn, F. and F. Strodtbeck (1961), *Variations in Value Orientations*, Evanston, IL: Greenwood Press.

Nahal, Anita (2005), 'Cultural collisions', *Diverse Issues in Higher Education*, **22**(20).

Phatak, A.V. (1983), *International Dimensions of Management*, Boston, MA: Kent.

Pincas, Anita (2001), 'Culture, cognition and communication in global education', *Distance Education*, **22**(1): 30–51.

Schein, E.H. (1985), *Organizational Culture and Leadership*, San Francisco, CA: Jossey-Bass.

Schneider, S.C. and J.-L. Barsoux (1997), *Managing Across Cultures*, Hemel Hempstead: Prentice Hall.

Sinclair, Amanda and Valerie Britton Wilson (1999), *The Culture-Inclusive Classroom*, Melbourne: Melbourne Business School, University of Melbourne.

Triandis, H.C. (1972), *The Analysis of Subjective Culture*, New York: Wiley, Interscience.

Trompenaars, F. and C. Hampden-Turner (2002), *Riding the Waves of Culture* (2nd edition), London: Nicholas Brearley.

3. Culture shock and cultural adjustment

David Killick*

If there's nothing wrong with me . . . maybe there's something wrong with the universe! Dr Crusher, *Star Trek: The Next Generation*. (Sheldon 1990)

All individuals crossing cultures face some common challenges as they pioneer lives of uprootedness and gradually establish working relationships with the new milieus. (Kim 2001: 5)

International students can become demoralised by early study experiences and even resentful of staff. They can lose confidence . . . [Some] may be mystified by new concepts and expectations such as independent study, 'critical thinking' and plagiarism. Most will become distressed if their attempts to master these new skills are unsuccessful. (Ryan 2000: 14)

When an international student travels to a new country, the journey he or she embarks upon is not simply a physical one. Tied to it are complex aspirations coming from the student and from his or her parents, extended family, teachers, sponsors and peers, along with expectations with regard to the new host culture (often outdated, stereotypical and inflated), and deep psychological links between one's own norms, values and established behaviours. As the familiar physical landscapes are replaced by those of the host culture, so are the familiar procedural schema (see Chapter 4) which guide us through every aspect of our daily routines from social contact to using public transport, from greeting our academic 'mentors' to opening a bank account. Of course, we know this will be the case at one level, but it is only the more explicit differences that we are prepared for, and even with these, as noted, expectations are often ill-grounded. Add to this the pressure of those many aspirations which the international student carries, and it is not difficult to appreciate why, as our 'existential security is threatened' (Stier 2003: 81), such disjuncture may have significant psychological impacts.

Research into the cross-cultural adjustment aspects of the international student experience can be summarized into two sets of factors (see Sandhu and Asrabadi 1994): the psychological 'intrapersonal' (for example feelings

* Leeds Metropolitan University.

of uncertainty, of homesickness, of loss of family and friends, and of inferiority compared to the home student community); and the social 'interpersonal' (for example weak language and social skills, absence of a trusted, understood, system of social support, practical difficulties in 'survival' in the host culture). These factors interrelate, and while culture shock is but one psychological impact it can be a significant inhibitor of effective adjustment.

The term 'culture shock' has been around since the 1960s (Oberg 1960). The topic is commonly covered in briefing and training sessions for business people embarking upon periods of work overseas and is supported by numerous 'self-help' guides (for example Marx 2001). The ease with which the term flows off the tongue has done it a disservice in some respects, as it rather diminishes the seriousness with which it is sometimes viewed. There has been a lot of discussion on the veracity of the classical U or W models of the phases of culture shock (see below), and some questioning of the uniqueness it is sometimes afforded (rather than seeing it as simply one example of the psychological process of adjustment which can affect people faced with a range of stressful events which generate new 'frames' or situations – those entering retirement, relocating to a new city or job, coming to terms with a chronic illness or new disability, for example). Nonetheless, the concept of culture shock provides a useful model for discussion with regard to the multicultural, multinational business class, with its own bases of accepted knowledge and procedures at odds with those of the newly arrived student:

> When people are exposed to knowledge differences, they can have intense emotional reactions. People spend a great deal of time and energy learning what their culture considers to be appropriate knowledge concerning how best to interact with others, how best to interview for jobs, and so forth. It is upsetting to discover that people from other cultures have very differing views concerning appropriate knowledge. (Brislin and Yoshida 1994: 124–5)

The 'shock' of culture shock really refers only to a specific aspect of the process of cultural adjustment (or 'cultural adaptation' or 'acculturation'),[1] which can be related overall to 'the degree of psychological comfort' (Kline Harrison et al. 1996: 169) which the student feels within the host culture.

In this chapter I will briefly outline the classic theory of culture shock before considering some theory relating to cultural adjustment insofar as this is relevant to business programmes serving the needs of diverse students. While the most common context for the discussion of culture shock has been that of the international sojourner, as implied above, the discussion is of equal relevance to any student whose cultural background has not prepared them for the 'norms' they will encounter in a university or on a particular course of studies, and the boundaries between 'culture shock' and 'learner shock' (Griffiths et al. 2005) blur in this context. While some research does indicate that international students experience greater adjustment difficulties than home students (see Snow Andrade 2006 for a summary), this has not focused on comparisons with, say, ethnic minority home students or those from poor socio-economic backgrounds – two groups which have higher than average attrition rates in the early period of their studies. What Stuart and Layer (2006: 2) note with regard to the UK is surely true of most universities in the 'developed' world:

> It is difficult to see that we should continue to treat 'international students' as a group in themselves distinct from 'home' students as the UK's student body has become so diverse. Culturally we are defining our student experience by the student's passport and fee status, but given the complexity of students' lives and experiences we should perhaps look at the picture differently.

Not surprisingly, perhaps, research by Pyvis and Chapman (2005) suggests that culture shock is also experienced by the growing number of students studying in a 'foreign' university based in their own country (transnational education). Like 'home' students on 'home' campuses, little attention is currently given to this dimension of their experience.

Institutions as well as individuals and nationalities also have cultures (see du Gay 1996 for discussions on the trend to generate business cultures). In universities some aspects of our institutional cultures are idiosyncratic – perhaps set by the presence of a dominant discipline, or a particular historical development, or a unique local recruitment demographic; and generic – let's say 'Anglophone-academic' though this is perhaps too vague to mean much, and I certainly can attest to exchange students travelling either way between the UK and both Australasia and North America encountering significant and unsettling differences in academic cultures. When the student meets the institution there is little compromise with regard to which culture is going to dominate the relationship.

Any aspect of a culture's values, attitudes, rituals, power structures and norms of behaviour can create borders, rifts and tensions which are difficult for the outsider to pinpoint and to navigate – and so they contribute to culture shock. For example, the chapter on cross-cultural capability (Chapter 4) provides an overview of some aspects of behaviour and cognition which may block effective cross-cultural communication, while discussions of dimensions of cultural difference in Chapter 2 outline some fundamental ways in which values may be differently assigned across cultures. The 'cultural iceberg' metaphor talks of difference above the water-line, such as behaviours, rituals or artefacts, and those below, such as beliefs and values, and postulates that it is the latter, hidden from view but always present, which have the most impact:

> Many, if not most, people think of culture as what is often called 'high culture' – art, literature, music, and the like. This culture is set in the framework of history and of social, political, and economic structures. . . . Actually, the most important part of culture for the sojourner is that which is internal and hidden . . . but which governs the behavior they encounter. This dimension of culture can be seen as an iceberg with the tip sticking above the water level of conscious awareness. By far the most significant part, however, is unconscious or below the water level of awareness and includes values and thought patterns. (Weaver 1993: 157)

The strain of having to live and function fully (the sojourner, not the tourist) amidst such confusion is the trigger for culture shock.

THE CLASSICAL MODEL

Oberg's classical model of culture shock proposes a U-shape of progression for the sojourner, starting on the left at something of a high point (the 'honeymoon' period when the new culture is 'interesting', 'exciting', 'exotic' and the traveller is 'curious' and in the mood for 'exploration' and 'discovery'). As time passes, however, the honeymoon mood is replaced by a deepening trough (culture shock in action) during which the sojourner may experience quite severe psychological and physiological impacts:

> Culture shock is seen as a temporary stress reaction where salient psychological and physical rewards are generally uncertain, and hence difficult to control or predict. Thus a person is anxious, confused and apparently apathetic until he or she has had time to develop a new set of cognitive constructs to understand and enact the appropriate behaviour. Writers about culture shock have often referred to individuals lacking points of reference, social norms and rules to guide their actions and understand others' behaviour. This is very similar to the attributes studied under the headings of alienation and anomie, which include powerlessness, meaninglessness, normlessness, self and social estrangement, and social isolation. In addition, ideas associated with anxiety pervade the culture shock literature. Observers have pointed to a continuous general 'free-floating' anxiety which affects people's normal behaviour. Lack of self-confidence, distrust of others and psychosomatic complaints are also common . . . Furthermore, people appear to lose their inventiveness and spontaneity, and become obsessively concerned with orderliness. (Furnham 1997: 15–16)

In most cases with the continuing passage of time, symptoms ease and adjustment occurs as the sojourner rises up the right-hand side of the U.

The extension to a W-shape accounts for the recurrence of the process as the sojourner returns to their own culture, changed by fresh perspectives, new experiences and an altered set of schema. All of which make 'reintegration' a similarly unsettling experience.

CULTURAL ADJUSTMENT

> So now it was dawning on some of the brighter ones that the only way people would accept vampires was if they stopped *being* vampires. That was a large price to pay for social acceptability, but perhaps not so large as the one that involved having your head cut off and your ashes scattered on the river. (Pratchett 2000)

Academia may be less direct in its reactions to difference than Pratchett's citizens of Ankh Morpork, but the pressure to conform to its established rituals and norms should not be dismissed lightly. Failures of many kinds may attenuate 'mal'adjustment: assignment failure, social failure or a sense of personal failure. We may argue that our general requirement is only for conformity to established practices, and not that students should stop being themselves. However, it may be that the rise from the bottom of the U-curve appears achievable only by a rejection of previous norms, values and behaviours, a process which is likely to be accompanied by a loss of personal identity and a high level of emotional stress, perhaps far more intimidating than the culture shock itself. Looking at reactions to adjustment stress, Ward et al. (2001: 71) propose that: 'Both stress and coping are mediated by characteristics of the individual and characteristics of the situation, and, in turn, affect adjustive outcomes'. Both dimensions are explored more fully below.

In this context, it is important to reflect upon the international student specifically as an individual prior to his or her arrival in our class, since they have a personal identity based (in the majority of cases) upon significant success: 'International students who come to the UK to study are successful learners; they have completed their previous studies in their home country satisfactorily and have been accepted onto a place at a UK university. Their strategies for learning have stood them in good stead' (Forland 2006: 3). Such a positive self-identity may actually make the initial phases of adjustment harder, as tried and tested learning strategies appear less effective, and success more elusive, conflicting with the student's self-image. On the other hand, such learners may have well-developed psychological or cognitive resources to draw upon to ease their eventual adjustment, and there is evidence of the importance a strong self-image can have in the process of cultural adaptation. For example, Yang et al. (2005) conclude that both 'independent self-construal' and language self-confidence (not necessarily language ability) are important factors in predicting successful adjustment to the new context.

There are many models of cultural adjustment, and between them a range of variables posited for what may facilitate or block such adjustment. The Milton Bennett (1998, 1993) model of 'intercultural sensitivity' seeks to analyse where an individual sits on a cline of sensitivity and then to guide a trainer in devising a programme to enable progression. This chapter is not intended to describe training principles or materials,[2] but Bennett provides an interesting starting point for considering the phases of cultural adjustment which may be experienced by a student. Bennett's model proposes two major positions with regard to cultural sensitivity: the 'ethnocentric' and the 'ethnorelative', each with three stages of progression. In the ethnocentric position, as the term implies, one's own culture forms the lens through which the world is seen (and understood, and judged). When submerged in cultural contexts removed from our own, such ethnocentric or xenophobic views are prone to be accentuated rather than diminished (Gudykunst and Kim 1997). One reason for this is the sheer volume of new information which has to be assimilated:

> As we go about collecting this vast amount of information, it is difficult to know what elements are key to understanding and navigating within that new culture. As human beings, our inclination is to focus on those things most important in our own cultures, most different from our own cultures, or most *obvious or easily* identifiable in the other culture. This often leads us to a rather superficial or ethnocentric analysis. (Phillips and Boyacigiller 2003: 77)

The watershed shift to the ethnorelative position enables one to see one's own culture in the light of another or others. Bennett's model proposes that an individual's sensitivity 'index' will be at different points according to the issue at hand and how they are feeling on that particular day or in that specific context. I would argue that successful cultural adjustment is dependent upon strong ethnorelative cultural sensitivity.

Paige (1993b) argues that any intercultural experience is one of 'psychological intensity', and poses 15 hypotheses with regard to features of the experience and the individual which will heighten the intensity. These can be summarized as:

1. The greater the degree of cultural difference between own and target cultures.
2. The more negatively the sojourner evaluates the cultural differences.
3. The more ethnocentric the sojourner.
4. The more ethnocentric the target culture.

5.   The more racist, sexist and in other ways prejudiced the target culture.
6.   The less the sojourner's language ability.
7.   The more essential language ability is in order to function in the target culture.
8.   The more the sojourner is immersed in the target culture.
9.   The less access the sojourners have to their own culture group.
10. The less the amount of prior, in-depth intercultural experience.
11. The more unrealistic the sojourner's expectations of the host culture.
12. Being physically different and feeling highly visible in the target culture.
13. Feeling invisible to the target culture because its members cannot accept important aspects of the sojourner's identity.
14. Feeling you are not getting the respect deserved, or are receiving undeserved recognition.
15. The less power and control one possesses in the intercultural situation.

Diminishing the intensity of the experience may assist with the process of adjustment, and some measures which we may take to do so are suggested later in this chapter.

Looking at the adaptation of longer-term migrants, Kim (1998) proposed four aspects which impact on the process,[3] summarized and modified by Martin (1994) to fit more closely the experience of the international student, these are:

● The sojourner's adaptive predisposition.
● The environmental receptivity.
● The communication of the sojourner with the host members.
● The specific outcomes of adaptation, including an enhanced sense of intercultural identity, psychological health and functional fitness. (Martin 1994: 13)

Kim proposes that the first three elements will determine the outcomes of the adaptation process, though as an ongoing process, a strong intercultural identity, good psychological health and functional fitness at any one time will create a virtuous circle of feedback into the other aspects. Adaptive predisposition is linked to personality (open-mindedness, flexibility, and so on) and to cultural background, in particular the degree of similarity between the student's and the host cultures. As noted elsewhere in this chapter, a student's expectations of the host culture have been shown to be an important variable when considering actual differences. Two factors within the host environment are suggested to be of significance: how receptive the host culture is towards the 'incomers',[4] and how great is the general level of pressure to 'conform' to social norms (more 'liberal' societies may be more likely to 'allow for' deviations from accepted behaviour by the sojourner). The ability to communicate effectively with the host community is suggested to play a significant role in adaptation to the new environment. As I suggest in Chapter 4 on cross-cultural capability in this volume, this goes far beyond 'language' skills as commonly understood, and is a dimension in which the host community plays a crucial part. In this context, however, it seems also to be important that sojourners maintain communication with home and/or members of their own culture as well as interacting with the host culture during their sojourn.

Stier (2003) provides a useful overview of the competences which constitute 'intercultural competence'. I summarize these below.

CONTENT COMPETENCIES (KNOWING 'THAT')

This is the knowledge we already have of a culture (in this case, the culture of the country or region of our sojourn and that of the academic community). This refers to its ways of doing things, the things it values, the people who inhabit its spaces, the signs and symbols it uses and the importance it attaches to them, its language, and so on. It is relevant to highlight that while very important, language itself is only one a series of knowledge sets, as evidenced by the culture shock which Australian students often experience when on exchange programmes in the UK, for example. It is commonly held that such knowledge of another culture can only be meaningful when we have a critical appreciation of ourselves as cultural beings and thereby of the culture we ourselves inhabit. Without this the knowledge is superficial, tends to stereotype and remains uncritically ethnocentric.

PROCESS COMPETENCES (KNOWING 'HOW')

Much of the 'knowing how' dimensions of intercultural competence correspond to the interpersonal competencies which generally make for an effective communicator, team member, socialite, and so on. These 'interpersonal' competencies (sensitivity to context and other participants, communicative competence, awareness of how others might see us, and so on) are highlighted in intercultural contexts because of the differences in the 'rules' which govern behaviour in the new culture (a simple example would be how do we know when it is our 'turn' in a conversation, and how can we interrupt if another person is speaking? The consequences of getting this wrong in terms of people's perceptions of us are significant in all cultures, and may be more so if our behaviour echoes an already established stereotype that 'all Anglorians are rude'). In addition to these interpersonal competencies, effective intercultural adjustment demands a series of intrapersonal competencies. These would include, crucially, the ability to step into the shoes of the 'other', and to reflect upon what is seen – bearing in mind what are the norms of the culture. To be effective, it is also necessary to be able to step back emotionally when one's own feelings are stirred in a particular intercultural incident, drawing upon what one knows about culture generally and about cultures in particular to take a more analytical stance, being reflective and recognizing that the real and often powerful feelings stirring within are based upon a lack of personal flexibility and a set of schema limited by one's own cultural norms. (A simplistic example would be the reaction to particular dishes based on ingredients considered inedible in one's own culture; a more complex example would be a feeling of disgust when confronted by a female lecturer with bare arms.)

Similarly, Yang et al. (2005) helpfully summarize factors impacting upon the 'psychological (emotional/affective)' and 'sociocultural (behavioural)' dimensions of 'cross-cultural adjustment':

> Psychological adjustment is postulated to be broadly affected by personality, life changes, coping styles, satisfaction/identification with co-nationals, and social support from co/host nationals . . . sociocultural adjustment is claimed to be best predicted by length of residence in the new culture, language ability, cultural knowledge, cultural distance, and the quantity of contact with host nationals. (Yang et al. 2005: 448)

As mentioned earlier, personality factors such as self-confidence, and an independent 'self-construal' (Oguri and Gudykunst 2002) (that is, how independent one perceives oneself to be, shaped through one's own culture or socialization) are believed to have a significant impact upon an individual's propensity for successful cultural adjustment. As personality factors like self-confidence are not culture-specific, this should warn us against any established stereotypes as to how likely, say, 'the Chinese' are to suffer deeply from culture shock or to find difficulties in making transitions into academic life. However, as self-construals are culture-mediated, it is likely that where two cultures evidence, recognize and reward, say, 'independence' similarly, those crossing between them may find adaptation partially eased compared to those crossing between cultures less similar in this regard, for example.

FACILITATING THE PROCESS OF ADAPTATION

[Academics] . . . can create particularly painful dilemmas for students from differing backgrounds, of differing turns of mind whose identities and loyalties are cast as liabilities from which they should liberate themselves. (Minnich 2005: 161)

It is (hopefully) unlikely that any of us so wish to compromise our students, but to escape such outcomes we need to become critical observers of our own practice, and to be sufficiently confident and flexible ourselves to adapt (and adopt) more inclusive approaches at the institutional level and within our individual lecture halls or tutorial rooms. Many universities or those departments within universities which have come to serve the needs of large numbers of international students have put various mechanisms in place to try and ease students into their new lives. Unfortunately these are sometimes minimalist and only rarely integrated into the learning experience (and again worth noting here is that they are in general only available to international students). Such a limited response is surprising if for no other reason than the economic and reputation loss of poor attainment and/or high attrition rates.

The most common intervention will be an orientation programme served up during the first week or so of arrival, possibly covering how to deal with culture shock, academic conventions and study skills, and navigating the local environment, for example. Given the U-curve theory, one immediate weakness with such programmes occurring only during the induction programme is that students in their honeymoon period (like newly-weds) are hardly receptive to those telling them that things will quickly deteriorate. Similarly, those whose self-identity is one of a successful learner and who have as yet no experience of trying to work within the host culture, are not best motivated to adopt new approaches to their learning. Research by McKinlay et al. (1996) actually found learners who had undertaken an orientation course, 'were significantly more homesick and reported more psychological difficulties' when compared with a group who had not attended the programme. This is not, I stress, to decry the practice of providing orientation courses, but is to argue that institutions and departments are being naive and/or neglectful if they think such front-loaded input is in itself sufficient (see McKinlay et al. 1996 for recommendations on more robust and effective support systems). Intercultural learning can and should be a two-way flow; the way we work with our students throughout their programme of study can be informed and enriched if we are willing to be as adaptable as we expect our (international) students to be.

The previous section indicated that attributes of the sojourner and attributes of the host culture play a part in the 'psychological intensity' of intercultural experiences. We might assume that ameliorating the degree of intensity of the experiences will ease the process of adjustment. Clearly, as academic staff within a university we can have most direct influence on the factors associated with the host culture, though this does not mean we cannot also help with some of the intrapersonal and interpersonal factors, too. Taking Paige's 15 parameters, I add a few suggestions for ways in which we may help in Table 3.1.

THE 'HOME' STUDENT

> By being explicit about the diversity that is in the room and acknowledging that we may *all* experience difficulties and frustrations, people can be encouraged to learn, through dialogue, about their differences and similarities. (Trahar 2007: 24)

This book focuses on the international student, and I have mentioned in passing that the issues raised in this chapter are equally, though perhaps differently, applicable to local students whose cultural background does not mirror that of the academic community they are joining. As with my comments in the chapter on cross-cultural capability, I would also wish to raise here the prospect that the students from 'other' cultures who successfully overcome culture shock and adjust to the new culture through the acquisition of intercultural competencies, take with them personal qualities and skills which will serve them well throughout their lives in both personal and professional spheres: 'as a result of significant experience in a culture other than one's own, there is an increase in world-mindedness, a reduction in ethnocentrism and the use of negative stereotypes, and greater sophistication in one's thinking about others' (Cushner and Mahon 2002: 47). The ways in which we facilitate cultural adjustment for the 'visiting' students (broader pedagogy, structured integration with the home student community, developing an ethos of openness, acceptance and curiosity, a more international curriculum content, better developed 'international' English and communication skills, and so on), will also serve our more traditional 'home' students well in broadening their horizons. Any additional experiential learning involving crossing cultures may also be greatly beneficial. Participating in international exchange, study abroad, volunteering or internship programmes are very clearly relevant here, but we must recognize that only a minority of students are likely to be able and willing to undertake these activities, so business courses should be seeking other innovative ways to get all their students to engage in challenging intercultural experiences. Ideally, in developing our higher education practice in

Table 3.1   Suggestions for ameliorating the impacts of cultural differences

Parameters which may impact on cultural adjustment (from Paige)	Possible interventions
1. The greater the degree of cultural difference between own and target cultures	• More flexible assessment criteria • Constantly critiquing our academic orthodoxy • Better understanding by academic staff of cultural differences in approaches to learning • Employing a wide range of pedagogic styles and techniques • Availability of culturally familiar things, such as refectory food (etc.)
2. The more negatively the sojourner evaluates the cultural differences	• Opportunities for 'deeper' engagement with the host community; more genuine integration
3. The more ethnocentric the sojourner 4. The more ethnocentric the target culture 5. The more racist, sexist, and in other ways prejudiced the target culture	• An institutional ethos in which ethnocentrism is challenged (across the whole student/staff body) • Vigilance and intolerance towards any form of racist, sexist, non-inclusive behaviour • Celebrations of cultural difference, cultural festivals, etc. open to the whole student community
6. The less the sojourner's language ability 7. The more essential language ability is in order to function in the target culture	• Language support for 'non-native' speakers. • More effective communication skills in English by staff and the 'native speaker community • Good learning support materials (e.g. notes for lectures, etc.) • Where possible, not penalising weak language skills in assessments (recognising the value of content, devising assessments which are less reliant on high-level language skills)
8. The more the sojourner is immersed in the target culture	• Good links to local faith groups, nationality clubs, etc.

Table 3.1   (continued)

Parameters which may impact on cultural adjustment (from Paige)	Possible interventions
9. The less access the sojourners have to their own culture group	• Nationality clubs/societies within the university • Staff body more representative of the students' cultures • Encouraging participation in other types of groups which provide a different kind of cultural affiliation (e.g. sports, music)
10. The less the amount of prior, in-depth intercultural experience	• While not 'prior', establishing at an early stage highly structured experiential cross-cultural contact through (for example) multicultural group work
11. The more unrealistic the sojourner's expectations of the host culture	• Honest and detailed pre-arrival information available to inbound students. • Pre-arrival link-up with student 'buddies'
12. Being physically different and feeling highly visible in the target culture	• Recruit a highly diverse staff/student population • Campus, prospectus, web images, course materials and references show wide diversity
13. Feeling invisible to the target culture because its members cannot accept important aspects of the sojourner's identity	• Cross-cultural capability development across the staff and student body • International/multicultural perspectives prominent within the curriculum
14. Feeling you are not getting the respect deserved, or are receiving undeserved recognition	• Ensuring cross-cultural group work is well structured,with assigned roles which rotate over time • Ensuring student representatives on course committees etc. seek out the views of 'minority' students • Being alert to preferred feedback/questioning behaviours across diverse student body
15. The less power and control one possesses in the intercultural situation	

this context, we can develop a balance between too much disjunction for 'other' culture students, and too little disjunction for stay-at-home 'majority' culture students. McNamee and Faulkner (2001), in discussing the impact of academic staff exchanges, echo this: 'too little meaning disruption is likely to result in little or no personal or professional growth. Too much meaning disruption, on the other hand, may be debilitating and interfere with the quality of the experience' (2001: 76). Kim (1998) and others have proposed that a sojourner's adjustment can be helped by predeparture training which raises awareness of culture shock, culture and cultural difference, oneself as a cultural being, and so on, and also helps set realistic views of the host culture. While not generally of relevance to how we can help our inbound students, such awareness-raising could be very helpful for outbound students, and also for students being placed in intercultural study groups or local multicultural work placements.

CONCLUSION

Culture shock is a natural reaction to a specific change in life circumstances. In the context of international students studying at university, it is in part generated by the new cultural setting of the host country, but also by the norms and expectations of the new 'culture' of learning. To this extent, home students as well as international students may undergo the stresses which it generates, as may those studying on a foreign campus or for a foreign award in their home country. Successful adjustment is partially dependent upon personality factors, and requires both psychological and behavioural changes. Adjustment may be eased by modifications within the host environment. More inclusive learning, teaching and assessment strategies, including well-structured cross-cultural integration within a course and across the institution, may serve to ease adjustment and at the same time to develop intercultural competences within the majority home student population. A developed awareness of one's own culture and its impact upon behaviours and values is crucial to the intercultural competencies required of students for successful cross-cultural adjustment and of those teaching multinational and multicultural groups if they are to meet student needs.

NOTES

1. I use the term 'adjustment' because I believe it better describes the changes which can enable the sojourner to participate successfully in the new context without changing

their 'self'. There is a psychological adjustment to being 'comfortable' within the new context, but not necessarily any change in underpinning values; behaviours are adapted in response to the demands of the new culture, but one's own are not abandoned. This is a weak version of what I think may be implied in notions of 'adaptation' or 'acculturation'.
2. See Bennett's Intercultural Communication Institute if interested: http://www.intercultural.org/
3. Kim later proposed a modified model for long-term 'enculturation' which included the important additional element of 'the strength of the strangers' ethnic group within the new environment' (Kim 2001: 147).
4. It is worth noting here that studies from a variety of sources in the UK 'are all consistent in demonstrating that international students both value the opportunity to meet and make friends with UK students while living in the UK and are more satisfied where this is the case' (Thom 2006: 6), yet only about a third had friends in the UK student population, and only about a third of UK students saw value in having international students as peers.

REFERENCES

Althen, G. (ed.) (1994), *Learning Across Cultures*, Washington, DC: NAFSA.
Bennett, M.J. (1986), 'A developmental approach to training for intercultural sensitivity', *International Journal of Intercultural Relations*, **10**(2): 179–95.
Bennett, M.J. (1993), 'Towards ethnorelativism: a developmental model of intercultural sensitivity', in R.M. Paige (ed.), *Education for the Intercultural Experience*, Yarmouth, ME: Intercultural Press, pp. 21–71.
Bennett, M.J. (ed.) (1998), *Basic Concepts in Intercultural Communication*, Yarmouth, ME: Intercultural Press.
Boyacigiller, N.A., R.A. Goodman and M.E. Phillips (eds) (2003), *Crossing Cultures: Insights from Master Teachers*, New York: Routledge.
Brislin, R.W. and T. Yoshida (1994), *Intercultural Communication Training: An Introduction*, London: Sage.
Cushner, K. and J. Mahon (2002), 'Overseas student teaching: affecting personal, professional, and global competencies in an age of globalisation', *Journal of Studies in International Education*, **6**(1): 44–58.
du Gay, P. (1996), 'Organizing identity: entrepreneurial governance and public management', in S. Hall and P. du Gay (eds), *Questions of Cultural Identity*, London: Sage, pp. 151–69.
Forland, H. (2006), 'The international student learning experience: bridging the gap between rhetoric and reality', *Going Global 2*, Edinburgh: British Council.
Furnham, A. (1997), 'The experience of being an overseas student', in D. MacNamara and R. Harris (eds), *Overseas Students in Higher Education: Issues in Teaching and Learning*, London: Routledge, pp. 14–29.
Griffiths, D.S., D. Winstanley and G. Yiannis (2005), 'Learning shock: the trauma of return to formal learning', *Management Learning*, **36**(3): 275–97.
Gudykunst, W. and Y.Y. Kim (1997), *Communicating with Strangers: An Approach to Intercultural Communication*, 3rd edn, New York: McGraw-Hill.
Hall, S. and P. du Gay (eds) (1996), *Questions of Cultural Identity*, London: Sage.
Kim, Y.Y. (1998), *Communication and Cross-Cultural Adaptation*, Philadelphia, PA: Multilingual Matters.
Kim, Y.Y. (2001), *An Integrative Theory of Communication and Cross-Cultural Adaptation*, London: Sage.

Kline Harrison, J., M. Chadwick and M. Scales (1996), 'The relationship between cross-cultural adjustment and the personality variables of self-efficacy and self-monitoring', *International Journal of Intercultural Relations*, **20**(2): 167–88.

Martin, J. (1994), 'Intercultural communication: a unifying concept for international education', in G. Althen (ed.), *Learning Across Cultures*, Washington, DC: NAFSA, pp. 9–30.

Marx, E. (2001), *Breaking Through Culture Shock: What You Need to Succeed in International Business*, London: Nicholas Brearley.

McKinlay, N.J., H.M. Pattison and H. Gross (1996), 'An exploratory investigation of the effects of a cultural orientation programme on the psychological well-being of international university students', *Higher Education*, **31**(3): 379–95.

McNamee, S.J. and G.L. Faulkner (2001), 'The international exchange experience and the social construction of meaning', *Journal of Studies in International Education*, **5**(1): 64–78.

Minnich, E.K. (2005), *Transforming Knowledge*, 2nd edn, Philadelphia, PA: Temple University Press.

Oberg, K. (1960), 'Culture shock: adjustment to new cultural environments', *Practical Anthropology*, **7**: 177–82.

Oguri, M. and W.B. Gudykunst (2002), 'The influence of self-construals and communication styles on sojourners', *International Journal of Intercultural Relations*, **26**: 577–93.

Paige, R.M. (ed.) (1993a), *Education for the Intercultural Experience*, Yarmouth, ME: Intercultural Press.

Paige, R.M. (1993b), 'On the nature of intercultural experiences and intercultural education', in R.M. Paige (ed.), *Education for the Intercultural Experience*, Yarmouth, ME: Intercultural Press, pp. 1–19.

Phillips, M.E. and N.A. Boyacigiller (2003), 'Cultural scanning: an integrated cultural framework approach', in N.A. Boyacigiller, R.A. Goodman and M.E. Phillips (eds), *Crossing Cultures: Insights from Master Teachers*, New York: Routledge, pp. 76–88.

Pratchett, T. (2000), *The Truth*, London: Corgi Books.

Pyvis, D. and A. Chapman (2005), 'Culture shock and the international student offshore', *Journal of Research in International Education*, **4**(1): 23–42.

Ryan, J. (2000), *A Guide to Teaching International Students*, Oxford: OCSLD.

Sandhu, D. and B. Asrabadi (1994), 'Development of an accumulative stress scale for international students: preliminary findings', *Psychological Reports*, **75**: 435–43.

Sheldon, L. (1990), 'Remember Me', *Star Trek: The Next Generation*, episode no. 79.

Snow Andrade, M. (2006), 'International students in English-speaking universities: adjustment factors', *Journal of Research in International Education*, **5**(2): 131–54.

Stier, J. (2003), 'Internationalisation, ethnic diversity and the acquisition of intercultural competencies', *Intercultural Education*, **14**(1): 77–91.

Stuart, M. and G. Layer (2006), 'Global connections: new thinking in institutional practice', *Going Global 2*, Edinburgh: British Council.

Thom, V. (2006), 'Enhancing the student experience: global education and integration', *Going Global 2*, Edinburgh: British Council.

Trahar, S. (2007), *Teaching and Learning: The International Higher Education Landscape*, Bristol: The Higher Education Academy, Subject Centre for Education, Discussions in Education Series, www.escalate.ac.uk/3559, accessed 8 July 2007.

Ward, C., S. Bochner and A. Furnham (2001), *The Psychology of Culture Shock*, London: Routledge.

Weaver, G.R. (1993), 'Understanding and coping with cultural adjustment stress', in Paige, R.M. (ed.), *Education for the Intercultural Experience*, Yarmouth, ME: Intercultural Press, pp.137–67.

Yang, R.P., K.A. Noels and K.D. Saumure (2005), 'Multiple routes to cross-cultural adaptation for international students: mapping the paths between self-construals, English language confidence, and adjustments', *International Journal of Intercultural Relations*, **30**: 487–506.

4. Cross-cultural capability: blocks to effective communication

David Killick*

INTRODUCTION

We see the world not as it is but as we are. (Variously attributed)

Do not do unto others as you expect they should do unto you. Their tastes may not be the same. (George Bernard Shaw 1903)

Diversity in our students, and across our colleagues, has the potential to transform the perspectives and capabilities of both ourselves and our students. It also has the potential to reinforce stereotypes and prejudices, and to make us more insular in our general outlook on the world. Within our classrooms and institutions it is the 'quality of intercultural contacts rather than the quantity' (Otten 2003) which we need to focus upon; our capacity and willingness to generate meaningful opportunities for genuine cross-cultural interaction[1] in our teaching and learning strategies are key to transforming the student experience and the outcomes of that experience from the 'naturally' ethnocentric to the 'enlightened' ethnorelative. There are many dimensions to this, but one of the keys to unlock the door of insularity is effective communication, as any successful business strategy would affirm. Communication, as we know, is at the very least a two-way process, and all participants in the communication process need to take responsibility for its effectiveness, and to develop the personal skills, attitudes and attributes which help ensure communication is effective – in both directions.

I use the term 'cross-cultural capability' to refer to those attributes which enable people to live (work, play, socialize, and so on) successfully with peoples of other cultures. Cross-cultural capability, therefore, includes not only knowledge and skills, but also the values and attitudes which, put simply, motivate people to engage with others in a spirit of openness, responsibility and curiosity. This chapter focuses on one important aspect of cross-cultural capability: effective communication. It is presented here in

* Leeds Metropolitan University.

the context of a department of business studies, but is of increasing importance to all disciplines in a more globally connected world:

> If we inhabitants of the globe do not acquire an awareness of our mutual
> differences, knowledge of basic cultural variables, the skills to communicate
> effectively across boundaries and the will to do so, our world will be the worse
> for it. We need to communicate effectively with people who were raised in ways
> utterly unlike our own. (Hofstede et al. 2002: xviii)

In looking at the cultural and communication strategies of our 'other'
students, it is at least equally important to look to those of ourselves
and the dominant culture of the student body, without which, this complex
of cultures will itself 'avoid interrogation' and so mean that with regard to
our home students, 'the differences *within* groups are obscured' (Trahar
2007: 10).

The cultural basis for differences in the way we communicate may be
influenced by underlying attitudes or values (see Chapter 2 re Hofstede and
Trompenaars for example), or may be 'simply' habits formed and passed on
through generations or peer groups (Edward T. Hall 1977, for example,
posits 'high-context' and 'low-context' cultures where, respectively, much
remains unsaid in a message but is inferred from a common understanding
of context, or by contrast those cultures where the message is made much
more explicit within itself, with limited reliance on shared understanding of
the context). Such differences, as outlined below, are not limited to different
national cultures or languages.

Our international students are often cited as examples of poor communicators on the grounds of their English language abilities. Leaving aside
the fact that they are undertaking a course of higher education in a language which is not only foreign, but in many cases may not even be their
second language but their third or fourth, we would do well to reflect that
their more general capabilities as cross-cultural communicators are also in
the main much better developed than those of our native speaker students,
or, indeed, perhaps of ourselves.

This chapter will consider some of the major barriers to effective cross-
cultural communication in a business studies context, arguing that it is the
responsibility of us all to develop our capabilities, and that doing so is a
matter of personal and professional enrichment. I will build in part on
areas touched upon in Chapter 2 of this volume, and assume a general
understanding of the concept of 'culture' which recognizes that national
culture is only one of a complex of cultural influences and identities
which we all inhabit (others would include, for example, gender, age, socio-
economic background, ethnicity and religion). I start from the premise

that, while we need to guide and support our international students and those home students whose own cultures may have established different approaches to communication than the norms of our higher education communities, their very experience of operating within another culture is a source of personal growth: 'life abroad represents an extensive natural learning situation which stimulates many more aspects of learners' personalities than are usually catered for in educational institutions' (Murphy-Lejeune 2003: 101). By contrast, those whose cross-cultural capabilities may be most in need of development are likely to be more 'traditional' students, for whom there is little need or motivation in a traditional study environment to focus on this area of personal development, as well as ourselves as professionals in higher education with responsibilities to address the diverse needs of our students. Any student leaving higher education today who is not capable of interacting effectively across cultures is hardly able to lay claim to some of the most fundamental graduate attributes required in a globalizing world: critically evaluating diverse viewpoints, making informed responses to different perspectives, recognizing the validity of differing interpretations of 'truth', and so on.[2]

BARRIERS TO EFFECTIVE CROSS-CULTURAL COMMUNICATION

Consider any cross-cultural encounter – whether with someone of a different nationality, or of a different race, or gender, or age, or socioeconomic background and so on:

- Where are you likely to encounter difficulties?
- Where are they likely to encounter difficulties?

What follows is a brief response to these questions – and the areas discussed apply to both of the questions (and to each of the participants) above.

LANGUAGE

Among the population in general this is probably the most commonly cited barrier to communication with 'foreigners' generally, and academic and administrative staff in universities would probably agree. Observations of the successful interactions between international students of different first languages in English, however, should make us wonder where the barriers are being created. While estimates and projected trends differ in detail (see for example Kachru 1992 and Graddol 2006), it is clear that 'native' speakers of English are a minority of its total speakers globally. There are more conversations taking place at any moment involving non-native speakers in English than there are between native speakers. As native speakers we create communication blocks for non-native speakers in a number of ways. For example:

- Use of idiomatic expressions.
- Use of phrasal verbs rather than lexical verbs.[3]
- Use of culture-specific references (see also the section below on schema).
- Use of irony or sarcasm.
- Reliance on intonation to indicate the function or the emphasis of an utterance.[4]

As native speakers we also tend not to be good at negotiating differences in the larger structuring of language – the ways in which discourse may be organized. In terms of verbal communication styles, for example, Gudykunst and Ting-Toomey (1988) elaborated four dimensions for variability:

- Directness – Indirectness.
- Elaborated – Exact – Succinct.
- Personal – Contextual.
- Instrumental – Affective.

Our own style, of course, will shift dependent on circumstances (who we are speaking to, the topic, the setting, and so forth). Nonetheless, communicative effectiveness is reduced where our interactions are with those whose 'normal' style lies elsewhere on one or more of these dimensions, and neither party is skilled at adjustment. This can lead us to consider them impolite, to judge serious content as flippant or vice versa, to fail to get the central point of their message, or to think they are 'waffling', for example. And, just to reiterate, our own style may well lead them to similar conclusions.

In a similar way (but possibly different ways), written communication also conforms to culturally specific norms in style. This may surface when we are grading assignments or presentations from students from cultures whose own discourse conventions favour, for example, a discursive circular response to a question rather than the linear 'progressive' structure demanded by Anglophone[5] academic traditions. We may choose to deal with this by educating ourselves better about alternative discourse styles, or by providing detailed guidance and practice opportunities in our own tradition. What often happens, though, is that neither of these takes place and students are penalized because the lecturer is unable to value the content of the submitted work through an inability to negotiate the 'style' in which it is presented.

Learning to monitor how we use our own language and to moderate for an international audience is an essential skill for English speakers. The fact that most international business is conducted in English already puts us at some disadvantage, heightened by our tendency to be poor at other languages. To compound this with an inability to speak something approaching an international variety of English is highly disrespectful, lazy and likely to cause frustration, lack of comprehension and loss of confidence among those we are dealing with. This is hardly a good starting point for effective cross-cultural communication or a trusting business partnership.

A significant barrier for international students studying with us, therefore, may be language skills. But the poor skills may lie with the native speaker community, including academic and administrative staff, as much as with the speakers of English as a foreign or second language.

NON-VERBAL COMMUNICATION (NVC)

It is often claimed, though probably impossible to substantiate, that between 60 and 90 per cent of face-to-face communication takes place non-verbally. Mehrabian (1971) famously attributed 7 per cent to words, 38 per cent to tone of voice and 55 per cent to use of body. Even if such figures are not applicable in all interaction contexts, NVC has a significant impact on the way any message is received and interpreted, and the seeds of mistrust or misunderstanding may well have been set before the verbal message itself is even transmitted. NVC may be explicitly taught in some business degrees, and aspects will certainly be covered in 'cultural briefings' for personnel heading off to exotic places to secure contracts. What follows, therefore, may be familiar. However, I would ask you to reflect upon the two-way nature of communication (verbal and non-verbal) as you consider some of the aspects of NVC covered below in relation to the diverse students within your class, and in relation to the skills development which could benefit those students disadvantaged by being stuck in their own cultural traditions while their international peers develop alongside them.

Whether based in underlying values or simply conforming to established patterns, NVC is very largely performed and registered subconsciously. Rather than diminish its impact, it is precisely because it exists below the 'waterline' (see Weaver 1993 for a commonly used analogy of the cultural awareness 'iceberg') that it can lead to highly emotive reactions when norms do not coincide (see Chapter 3 on culture shock for the impact of coping with sustained differences).

NVC ranges from the message we send or receive through our appearance (dress, make-up, pierced noses, cropped hair) and broader socially constructed extensions (choice of car, style of house and its furnishings, holiday destinations), through gestures to body language and our attitudes to time. Here I will look briefly on the last two, but we should not diminish the importance of the others; some common gestures in one culture can cause great offence (or confusion) when observed by members of another culture – the presence or absence of a tie or the exposure of an arm or leg can send very different messages and lead to loss of respect or feelings of distrust before any verbal communication has had a chance.

In addition to overt 'gesturing', the way we use our bodies to convey and interpret messages can be separated into specific aspects of NVC:

- Body language and posture – largely subconscious stances and positioning of the body (for example folded arms, downcast head or a shoulder shrug).
- Haptics – when, where and how we touch each other, and who we touch.
- Oculesics – when, where and how we make eye contact with each other, and with whom.
- Proxemics – how physically close we get to whom, when and where.
- Chronemics – our relationship with time, for example the importance we give to things like punctuality, how many tasks we perform at once, and whether time drives interactions more or less than personal relations.

Effective teaching and learning is dependent upon effective communication. We might spend years honing our lecturing skills, mastering the use of PowerPoint or a blackboard, and be dismayed to discover (if we are lucky enough to discover it) that six students from Fantasia have spent the whole semester so disturbed by the way we 'stare' at them that they feel too ashamed to hear a word of it. Meanwhile, the student from Plutopia who has diligently ensured throughout the year that he arrives for his tutorial 30 minutes early, as his customary cultural practice dictates, causes us such offence by his insistent early arrival and then by the way he lowers his head when questioned about his assignment that we subconsciously respond to his work, blocked initially by our feeling of irritation and subsequently by a feeling that he is being less than honest with us.

Other transgressions in norms of behaviour are equally likely to block or interfere with the transmission and reception of communication across cultures. Standing closer *or* more distantly than appropriate for the level of intimacy of the situation will stir feelings of discomfort. Touching 'inappropriately' may simultaneously cause some to feel harassed or under threat and others to feel they have been dealt with coldly. Cross-cultural capability would imply not that we are always able to get this right, but that we are aware of the potential impact our own actions may have and seek to be sensitive to this when in cross-cultural encounters, and at the same time that we monitor our own affective reactions to try to override emotions which may be stirring below our own waterline of consciousness.

It should be noted that institutions themselves also send out NVC messages 'which convey the institutional ethos' (Jones and Killick 2007: 110) through both overt symbols (logo, choice of illustrations in the prospectus or website and around campus), and more covert symbols (whether or not it is the norm for academic staff to have 'open doors' or rigid appointment slots, how students hand in their work, what is the expectation on attendance and punctuality, what is the standard form of address for students speaking to staff). As in all other aspects of NVC, these are often so familiar to those of us working within the institution that we fail to recognize that they are norms ('normal') only in the narrow context of that institution or particular educational tradition, and may send messages which others either fail to interpret or misinterpret, for either of which they may be penalized.

MISATTRIBUTION

Tourists stare at . . . [Moroccans] . . . in the Grand Soco, wondering, perhaps, what odd Johnnies they are, never suspecting that the scrutiny is reciprocal. With our sun-scorched foreheads, our bikini-in-the-street shamelessness, what can they think? (Michael Watkins, *The Times*, 19 March 1983, quoted in Storti 1990)

So far I have referred principally to our largely subconscious emotional responses to the cultural clashes we encounter, whether through linguistic, paralinguistic or non-verbal communication. Here we consider another type of reaction, which can occur when such responses are raised to the level of consciousness. In this context the term 'misattribution' can be applied to the process of (mis)attributing a set of values to observed behaviour(s). I will illustrate through the example of oculesics.

For Fantasians a very important value is that of modesty between the sexes. For Plutopians a very important value is that of respect for one's elders. For Anglorians a very important value is that of honesty in personal relations. (It is actually highly likely that all cultures share these values, though perhaps give different emphasis to one or other.) As everybody at this multicultural project planning meeting is following their cultural briefings, these values should present no difficulties to cross-cultural communication: in preparation, the Anglorian and Plutopian have covered their arms and legs, the Fantasian and Angolan have ensured the older Plutopian delegate has the chair at the head of the table, and the Fantasian and Plutopian delegates take care not speak to each other in their common language while the Anglorian is with them. So why does the Fantasian leave the meeting believing both others to be sexually aggressive, the Plutopian leave believing the others are disrespectful creatures, and the Anglorian think that neither of the others is trustworthy? Referring back to oculesics, our Fantasian exhibits his value of sexual modesty by avoiding eye contact with the two other female delegates, thereby apparently disrespecting the elder Plutopian whose culture requires youngers to 'look back when looked at' and appearing dishonest to his Anglorian counterpart for failing to make eye contact. The Anglorian exhibits her honesty by seeking out eye contact with everybody, thereby apparently exhibiting sexual wantonness to the Fantasian and again disrespecting the elder Plutopian whose culture requires youngers to 'look back only when looked at'. You can work out the Plutopian for yourself. If you think the example rather far-fetched, consider the stereotypes you hear ('xx are a shifty lot') and consider what they may be based upon.

STEREOTYPES

> Hath not a Jew eyes? Hath not a Jew hands, organs, dimensions, senses, affections, passions? (*The Merchant of Venice*)

Our stereotypes of others and theirs of us create filters, sometimes very dense ones, which obscure and/or alter the flows of communication. Consequently, we tend to decry stereotyping, and to disassociate it from our own sophisticated ways of understanding the world.

Cognitively, however, it appears that it is a very natural thing to form stereotypes: 'The concept of stereotype has gradually lost its earlier connotation of irrationality and prejudice; instead stereotyping is now considered an ordinary cognitive process in which people construct schemata to categorise people and entities in order to avoid "information overload"' (Guirdham 1999: 161). 'Other people' is simply a particular category for our mind to organize and process, as it does the world more generally (see Aitchison's 2003 'birdy birds' for discussion on prototype theory in linguistics for example, and the section below on schema).

Socially, stereotyping is based upon the existence of 'in-groups' and 'out-groups', and our perhaps very basic human need to belong to an in-group creates the concomitant need to differentiate those beyond that group. Stereotyping is one aspect of our propensity to ethnocentrism, whereby people 'judge others from their own culture's perspective, believing theirs to be the only "right" or "correct" way to perceive the world' (Cushner and Brislin 1996: 5). Not to stereotype is to deny the validity of our own sense of (group) identity; indeed even more fundamentally the 'other' is necessary for us, since our 'identities are constructed through, not outside, difference' (Hall 1996: 4). To assert that you do not have or believe in stereotypes is likely to reflect an intellectual aspiration rather than any objective reality. Even if you have somehow attained such a lofty stage of enlightenment, others around you probably have not.

Specific stereotypes, like other belief and value systems, are culturally transmitted, and quite pernicious in their ability to stick around despite oceans of conflicting evidence. It also seems to be common for stereotypes to lead to prejudices and these, in turn, to form the justification for discriminatory behaviour. While these, too, may be 'natural' the human social enterprise compels that we be armed to resist.

It is not uncommon in my experience to hear academics who in other contexts exercise very precise rigour to begin sentences with, 'International students are always . . .', or 'Chinese students never seem to . . .', for example. Notwithstanding the discussion above about the need to conform to the cultural norms of our 'in-group', we do well to remember that even students can be individuals. Just a moment's consideration of the first attempt above to generalize to stereotype indicates the total implausibility of completing the sentence with anything more meaningful than something tautological like, 'International students are always . . . from another country'. Nor is the stereotyping of particular nationalities of students by academics limited to casual remarks to colleagues, but can be found in research literature on learning styles and strategies which continue to inform approaches to teaching and learning in higher education (see De Vita 2007 for a critique of some of these). This obvious truth about the dangers of asserting and expecting international students to conform to stereotypes, of course, also applies to stereotypes we may hold or assert about all or any particular group of our 'home' students. At the start of this chapter and elsewhere there is reference to the complexity of our cultural identities – 'youth' culture may make our students across many nationalities less alien to each other than they are to some of us less youthful members of staff; a theist orientation may give a Pakistani Muslim student more points of contact with a Peruvian Catholic than with his secularist tutor.

Stereotyping, whether positive or negative, provides a mental short-cut to our interpretation of the world, but short-cuts often trap the unwary. Entering an encounter with somebody for whom we already have an unwritten set of assumptions is a great way to block effective cross-cultural communication. We should not, however, sink into denial about our propensity to stereotype. A capability to reflect upon the stereotypes which might accompany us into our encounters with students, and developing within all our students the same capability, would seem a prerequisite for effective business education and practice. Similarly, we should not be surprised or offended if others hold stereotypes of us, helping diffuse these can be difficult, but is also our responsibility if we are serious about wanting to communicate effectively.

In terms of facilitating learning and developing effective cross-cultural capabilities, it is also pertinent here to mention here the notion of stereotype threat (Steele and Aronson 1995). Research in this area suggests that where a stereotype is generally held (and is known to those being stereotyped), there will be a tendency to conform to its attributes. Black Americans' underperformance on IQ tests and women's underperformance in maths in the USA may be attributable to a self-belief in the likelihood of such underperformance, for example. This clearly has implications in our own context for those business students whose 'cultural' background means they are stereotyped as 'poor communicators' or 'insular' or 'rote learners', for example.

SCHEMA

> I have not yet learned to see an Indian village or a bazaar; my eyes aren't trained, and I couldn't describe one to save my life. I love them and am endlessly fascinated; but all I can make out is a wild surrealist confusion of men and animals and many kinds of inanimate objects, arranged in completely implausible patterns. (Taylor 1947)

The ways we make connections between knowledge, ideas, events, and so on depends in part upon the schemas[6] we develop through the processes of socialization, education, and so on, which shape our worldview. Such processes continue throughout our lives, and our schemas adapt in the light of experience; though the adage that old dogs cannot be taught new tricks indicates a limit to such development. Building from original work by Bartlett (1932), a schema refers to a mental representation of a part of the world. Like linguistic prototypes, or stereotypes in social psychology, schemas are posited in cognitive psychology as mental mechanisms which help us to process information and situations quickly, based upon our previous experience and knowledge of the world. A simple example of schema activated (or not) through language might be a lecture on supply chain management in which the lecturer illustrates the concept through reference to 'Big W'. While intended to help students, the 'Big W' reference will only facilitate mental processing for those students whose schema includes this particular brand; for others it forms a barrier to comprehension of the whole lecture.

Faced with new contexts our processing skills are somewhat slowed down and/or more prone to derive inaccurate assumptions. A very simple example of this would be how much easier it is to cross the road in a country where people drive on the same side as us. Processing the opposite traffic flow may only take micro-seconds longer, but that can literally make the difference between life and death. It is also our schema on academic writing conventions, for example, which enable us to process more quickly or more thoroughly the assignments submitted by those whose own writing schema correspond closely to our own (see Winskel n.d. for a very helpful presentation of different types of schema as they relate to academic discourse). By extension, we can see that this last point also better enables students from an Anglophone academic tradition to assimilate the bulk of the reading assigned in a course, the linear lectures delivered on a course, and the Socratic question and answering routine of a tutorial session.

Procedural schemas such as that needed for the tutorial help us in all kinds of daily routines – from using public transport to joining in with an established group at a coffee table. The schemas for full participation in academic life (or in international commerce) are complex and largely unspoken. Students faced with procedural schemas out of kilter with their own are likely to falter, to create poor impressions, to communicate 'inappropriately' or 'inadequately', and so forth. Or, once again to emphasize this point, staff faced with procedural schemas out of kilter with their own are likely to falter, to create poor impressions, to communicate 'inappropriately' or 'inadequately', and so forth. Experience of recognizing and adapting to different sets of schema is probably some measure of a rounded education and should create individuals with more flexibility, and with that a greater openness to novelty.

CONCLUSION

Cross-cultural communication is part of a broader set of capabilities which together enable our students and ourselves to engage more effectively, professionally and personally, in the modern border-crossing world. It is not restricted to communication across national or linguistic boundaries; our classrooms are full of diverse cultural groupings of many other kinds. These include pictures on our wall, the formality of our dress, the words we choose and the tone in which we use them, the choice to write or not write in the first person and the time it takes us to get to the point when presenting an argument, the way we make eye contact and the amount of physical contact we have, our stereotypes and the way in which we organize our worldview. Each of these impacts upon the messages we send and their interpretation. Our own awareness and openness in each of the above impacts equally upon the way we interpret the messages we receive. Effective cross-cultural communication depends upon high levels of flexibility across all these areas. It is not only arrogant, but also personally highly limiting for ourselves and our 'majority' students if we believe developing such flexibility is the sole responsibility of students whose cultural norms in these respects differ from those established within an Anglophone academic tradition.

NOTES

1. I use the term 'cross-cultural' as opposed to 'intercultural' although much of the literature will use the second term. The distinction is blurred, and the terms are inconsistently applied. In this chapter I take the view that 'cross-cultural' refers to communication between peoples of different cultures principally from positions outside of their respective cultures, whereas 'intercultural' has the implication of a more intimate relationship with the culture of the 'other'. In cross-cultural communication there is no agenda to 'acculturate' or become like the 'other', only the intent to understand and be understood as fully and as openly as possible.
2. By differing interpretations of 'truth' I am referring, for example, to the secular and the religious worldviews, or to the value placed upon the 'scientific' method, or to the 'Western' logic that a statement excludes its opposite: 'If A is true, B, which is the opposite of A, must be false', as opposed to 'Eastern' logic, whereby, 'If A is true, its opposite B may also be true, and together they produce a wisdom which is superior to either A or B' (Hofstede 1991: 171).
3. Think, for example, of the verb 'get' – as a phrasal verb this is linked in English to a large number of prepositions (up, round, over) and even multiple prepositions (round to, out of) to give it a unique meaning (respectively, the above combinations have a corresponding 'lexical verb': rise, avoid, recover, start doing, avoid doing). 'Get' is the most frequently occurring phrasal verb root, but many other verbs also have several combinations. You can imagine how difficult it is to get to grips with this when studying English as a foreign language.
4. As a simple example consider the statement, 'You're from Mexico.' Simply by adding a rising intonation this is transformed into a question: 'You're from Mexico?' Failure to respond may leave the tutor (or border guard) assuming the student is unable to understand the simplest English (so how could they possibly study here?). In fact the student assumes that this is a statement rather than a question. There is not room to consider the very complex uses of intonation in English here, but careful attention to what we say and how we say it can help us recognize where we may be confusing through a reliance on intonation. Use of intonation forms one part of the study of paralinguistics, which explores how meanings in spoken language are conveyed beyond words and syntax – for example through pitch, pauses, accent, and so on.

5. I choose to refer to 'Anglophone' as a shorthand here, and deliberately do not use 'Western' since, for one thing, those performing in a Francophone or Germanic context would be required to conform to very different norms. That said, conventions even between Anglophone academic cultures differ to some extent.
6. I use the singular term 'schema' and the plural 'schemas', though the plural 'schemata' is also commonly used. In some cases you will find 'schemata' used to describe the total schemas which form an individual's cognitive models.

REFERENCES

Aitchison, J. (2003), *Words in the Mind: An Introduction to the Mental Lexicon*, 3rd edn, Oxford: Blackwell.
Bartlett, F.C. (1932), *Remembering: An Experimental and Social Study*, Cambridge: Cambridge University Press.
Cushner, K. and R.W. Brislin (1996), *Intercultural Interactions: A Practical Guide*, 2nd edn, Thousand Oaks, CA: Sage.
De Vita, G. (2007), 'Taking stock: an appraisal of the literature on internationalising HE learning', in E. Jones and S. Brown (eds), *Internationalising Higher Education*, London: Routledge, pp. 154–67.
Graddol, D. (2006), 'English next: why global English may mean the end of English as a foreign language', British Council, http://www.britishcouncil.org/files/documents/learning-research-english-next.pdf, accessed 8 July 2007.
Gudykunst, W.B. and S. Ting-Toomey (1988), *Culture and Interpersonal Communication*, Newbury Park, CA: Sage.
Guirdham, M. (1999), *Communicating Across Cultures*, London: Macmillan.
Hall, E.T. (1977), *Beyond Culture*, Garden City, NY: Anchor Press/Doubleday.
Hall, S. (1996), 'Who needs "identity"?' in S. Hall and P. du Gay (eds), *Questions of Cultural Identity*, London: Sage, pp. 9–17.
Hofstede, G. (1991), *Culture and Organizations: Software of the Mind*, London: McGraw-Hill.
Hofstede, G.J., P.B. Pedersen and G. Hofstede (2002), *Exploring Culture*, Yarmouth, ME: Intercultural Press.
Jones, E. and D. Killick (2007), 'Internationalisation of the curriculum', in E. Jones and S. Brown (eds), *Internationalising Higher Education*, London: Oxon: Routledge, pp. 109–19.
Kachru, B.B. (1992), *The Other Tongue: English across Cultures*, Urbanz, IL: University of Illinois Press.
Mehrabian, A. (1971), *Silent Messages*, Belmont, CA: Wadsworth.
Murphy-Lejeune, E. (2003), 'An experience of interculturality: student travellers abroad', in G. Alred, M. Byram and M. Fleming (eds), *Intercultural Experience and Education*, Clevedon: Multilingual Matters, pp. 101–13.
Otten, M. (2003), 'Intercultural learning and diversity in higher education', *Journal of Studies in International Education*, **7**(1): 12–26.
Shaw, G.B. (1903), *Man and Superman*.
Steele, C.M. and J. Aronson (1995), 'Stereotype threat and the intellectual test performance of African Americans', *Journal of Personality and Social Psychology*, **69**(5): 797–811.
Storti, C. (1990), *The Art of Crossing Cultures*, Yarmouth, ME: Intercultural Press.
Taylor, E. (1947), *Richer by Asia*, Boston, MA: Houghton Mifflin Co.

Trahar, S. (2007), *Teaching and Learning: The International Higher Education Landscape*, The Higher Education Academy, Subject Centre for Education, Discussions in Education Series, www.escalate.ac.uk/3559, accessed 8 July 2007.

Weaver, G.R. (1993), 'Understanding and coping with cultural adjustment stress', in Paige, R.M. (ed.), *Education for the Intercultural Experience*, Yarmouth, ME: Intercultural Press, pp. 137–68.

Winskel, H. (n.d.), 'Application of schema theory to academic discourse: the summary writing process', http://www.latrobe.edu.au/lasu/conference/winskel. doc, accessed 8 July 2007.

5. Learning

Learning: n.1. Knowledge acquired by systematic study in any field or fields of scholarly application. 2. the act or process of acquiring knowledge or skill. (Macquarie Library 1981)

Learning is a complex process that has many facets to it depending on context, situation and purpose. The purpose of learning from a safety demonstration in a workplace is about saving life and limb. The purpose of learning in a university setting is about acquisition and enhancement of knowledge. In the context of a global multicultural classroom it becomes even more complex to recognise the cultural factors that affect the learnings of different people from different nations. Is learning what we, the educators deem to be appropriate to pass on to the student, or is learning what the student deems to be appropriate and absorbs from the educator?

This simple question is exacerbated once we take it into the higher education context of adult learning and of multicultural classrooms. Adult learning has quite different parameters to learning during early childhood or middle childhood and requires an understanding of the adult within the context of the world in which that adult lives and works. As a business educator facing a global, multicultural classroom, the complexity of adult learning takes on a whole new meaning as the student body represents multifaceted backgrounds of learning that may clash significantly within the classroom.

In this chapter we explore learning, adult learning, the history of adult learning, issues related to adult learning, and try to put this all in the context of multicultural classrooms. That is, we will glean from our collective knowledge and wisdom and apply this to the uniqueness of a classroom full of adults who have significantly different understandings of learning, teaching, the role of professors, the role of higher education, and their own expectations of themselves.

THEORIES OF LEARNING

Knowles et al. (2005) tell us that traditionally we have known more about how animals learn than about how children learn; and we know much more about how children learn than how adults learn. There is much debate about types of literature on learning theories and the various schools of thought about learning. Some contemporary thinking has two major families of learning theories: those that are behaviourist or connectionist theories, and the cognitive or gestalt theories (Knowles et al.). The delineation between the two families is based not only on differences within the theories but also upon specific issues which form the basis of differing theories. However, in terms of a discussion on diversity and adult learning the work of Reese and Overton (1970) is useful in terms of considering the elemental model and the holistic model.

The elemental model is essentially a machine model which represents the universe as a system composed of discrete pieces operating in a spatiotemporal field. This leads to a sequential model where all other more complex phenomena are reduced to a chain-like sequence which therefore leads to a concept in principle of complete predictability.

The holistic model represents the universe as a unitary, interactive, developing organism. The whole therefore is organic rather than mechanical. This model sees people as an active organism rather than a reactive organism, and represents groups of individuals as an organized entity.

From the holistic frame of thought has emerged the phenomenologist perspective as expressed by Coombs and Snygg in Pittenger and Gooding (1971):

- A person behaves in terms of what is real to him or her and what is related to himself or herself at the moment of action.
- Learning is a process of discovering one's personal relationship to and with people, things and ideas. The process results in and from a differentiation of the phenomenal field of the individual.
- Further differentiation of the phenomenological field occurs as an individual recognizes some inadequacy of a present organization. When a change is needed to maintain or enhance the phenomenal self, it is made by the individual as the right and proper thing to do. The role of the teacher is to facilitate the process.
- Given a healthy organism, positive environmental influences and a non-restrictive set of precepts of self, there appears to be no forseeable end to the perceptions possible for the individual.
- Transfer is a matter of taking current differentiations and using them as first approximations in the relationship of oneself to new situations.
- Learning is permanent to the extent that it generates problems that may be shared by others and to the degree that continued sharing itself is enhancing.

In the context of a business classroom with students of differing cultures and perspectives, the holistic model clearly relates as a more constructive and useful learning model as we attempt to encourage students to learn within the context of their own environment and their own world experience.

ADULT LEARNING

When we turn our attention to adult learning in particular it is interesting to observe that since the dawn of time all the great teachers – including Confucius, the Hebrew Prophets, Jesus, Aristotle, Plato, Socrates, Cicero, Quintilian and the Buddha – were teachers of adults, not teachers of children. Although from different times and different cultures, they all taught adults. Yet the field of adult education as a theoretical construct is not particularly well researched and developed, given the hundreds and thousands of years that have transpired since our early educators. It is these early educators such as the ancient Chinese and Hebrews that invented the case study method of learning, and the Greeks who invented what we now call the Socratic dialogue method of learning.

The early discourse on adult learning commenced from our understanding of teaching children. 'Pedagogy' means the art and science of teaching children and is founded on a set of beliefs, an ideology founded on assumptions about teaching and learning that evolved between the seventh and twelfth centuries in the monastic and cathedral schools of Europe. It would appear that an entire educational system covering all ages is founded on the pedagogical method. The result is that until recent times, adults have been taught as if they were children, with the decisions of what to learn and how to learn left entirely in the hands of the teacher.

Teacher-led education founded on these principles leads to the following pedagogical assumptions:

1. The need to know. How the learning applies to your life and the relevance of the learning to your life experiences is entirely subjugated to what the teacher has predetermined is needed to be known to attain a pass.
2. The learner's self-concept. The learner's self-concept is to become a dependent personality based on the teacher's concept that the learner depends on the teacher for all learning.
3. The role of experience. The fundamentals of pedagogical methodology are the teacher, books, teaching aids, and so forth, and the learner's experience is of no relevance to the learning process.

4. Readiness to learn. For a learner to pass they must learn what the teacher tells them they must learn.
5. Orientation to learning. Learning experiences are organized according to the subject matter content. This presumes a learner has a subject orientation to learning.
6. Motivation. Motivation to learn is from external motivators such as grades, parents, teacher approval. It does not allow for intrinsic motivators such as a commitment to lifelong learning.

As adults, the learning assumptions of pedagogy appear to lack significant credibility. As we consider the concept of who is an adult, we understand there are a number of ways of defining an adult. The biological perspective would be based on reaching the age of reproduction. The psychological perspective is based when we arrive at a self-concept of our capacity to become responsible for our own lives and of being self-directing. The legal perspective is founded on when the law says we are liable or responsible for certain actions; driving, paying full fare and voting are examples. Socially we become adults when we are deemed to be able to take on socially acceptable roles such as full-time work, or becoming a parent or spouse.

From an educational perspective it is the psychological context that determines and influences the development of adult education and moves from the concept of pedagogy to that of andragogy.

Mark Smith (1999) offers the following summation of the language of adult learning and of its terminology:

> The term andragogy was originally formulated by a German teacher, Alexander Kapp, in 1833. He used it to describe elements of Plato's education theory. Andragogy (andr- meaning 'man') could be contrasted with pedagogy (paed-meaning 'child' and agogos meaning 'leading') (see Davenport 1993: 114). Kapp's use of andragogy had some currency but it was disputed, and fell into disuse. It reappeared in 1921 in a report in which it was argued that 'adult education required special teachers, methods and philosophy, and the term andragogy was used to refer collectively to these special requirements. Eduard Lindeman was the Wrst writer in English to pick up on the use of the term. He only used it on two occasions. As Stewart, his biographer, comments, 'the new term seems to have impressed itself upon no one, not even its originators'. That may have been the case in North America, but in France, Yugoslavia and Holland the term was being used extensively to refer to the discipline which studies the adult education process or the science of adult education.

In this discussion the distinction between pedagogy and andragogy is explored and whilst there is considerable debate around these terminologies there is acceptance that adult education and adult learning is different in characteristic, style and construct to childhood learning.

Malcolm Knowles (1984) developed a framework for understanding adult learning and is widely regarded as a foremost thinker in this field. He identified that the characteristics of adult learners are fundamentally different to the characteristics of child learners. He presented five differing assumptions that underpin that difference:

1. Self-concept. As a person matures, his self-concept moves from one of being a dependent personality toward one of being a self-directed human being.
2. Experience. As a person matures, he accumulates a growing reservoir of experience that becomes an increasing resource for learning.
3. Readiness to learn. As a person matures, his readiness to learn becomes oriented increasingly to the developmental tasks of his social roles.
4. Orientation to learning. As a person matures, his time perspective changes from one of postponed application of knowledge, to immediacy of application. Accordingly his orientation toward learning shifts from one of subject-centredness to one of problem-centredness.
5. Motivation to learn. As a person matures, the motivation to learn is internal.

Mark Smith (1999) went on to say:

With these things in mind we can look at the assumptions that Knowles makes about adult learners:

1. Self-concept. As a person matures his self-concept moves from one of being a dependent personality toward one of being a self-directed human being. The point at which a person becomes an adult, according to Knowles, psychologically, 'is that point at which he perceives himself to be wholly self-directing. And at that point he also experiences a deep need to be perceived by others as being self-directing' (Knowles 1984: 56). As Brookfield (1986) points out, there is some confusion as to whether self-direction is meant here by Knowles to be an empirically verifiable indicator of adulthood. He does say explicitly that it is an assumption. This raises some interesting issues.

   ● Both Erikson and Piaget have argued that there are some elements of self-directedness in children's learning (Brookfield 1986: 93). Children are not dependent learners for much of the time, 'quite the contrary, learning for them is an activity which is natural and spontaneous' (Tennant 1988: 21). It may be that Knowles was using 'self-direction' in a particular way here or needed to ask a further question – 'dependent or independent with respect to what?'
   ● The concept is culturally bound – it arises out of a particular (humanist) discourse about the self which is largely North American in its expression.

2. Experience. As a person matures he accumulates a growing reservoir of experience that becomes an increasing resource for learning. This led to the belief that adults learn more effectively through experiential techniques of education such as discussion or problem solving (Knowles 1980: 43). The immediate problem we have is the unqualified way in which the statement is made. There may be times when experiential learning is not appropriate – such as when substantial amounts of new information are required. We have to ask the question, what is being learnt, before we can make such judgements.

  A second aspect here is whether children's and young people's experiences are any less real or less rich than those of adults. They may not have the accumulation of so many years, but the experiences they have are no less consuming, and still have to be returned to, entertained, and made sense of. Does the fact that they have 'less' supposed experience make any significant difference to the process? A reading of Dewey (1933) and the literature on reflection (e.g. Boud et al. 1985) would support the argument that age and amount of experience makes no educational difference. If this is correct, then the case for the distinctiveness of adult learning is seriously damaged. This is of fundamental significance if, as Brookfield (1986: 98) suggests, this second assumption of andragogy 'can arguably lay claim to be viewed as a "given" in the literature of adult learning'.

3. Readiness to learn. As a person matures his readiness to learn becomes oriented increasingly to the developmental tasks of his social roles. As Tennant (1988: 21–22) puts it, 'it is difficult to see how this assumption has any implication at all for the process of learning, let alone how this process should be differentially applied to adults and children'. Children also have to perform social roles.

  Knowles does, however, make some important points at this point about 'teachable' moments. The relevance of study or education becomes clear as it is needed to carry out a particular task. At this point more ground can be made as the subject seems relevant.

  However, there are other problems. These appear when he goes on to discuss the implications of the assumption. 'Adult education programs, therefore, should be organised around "life application" categories and sequenced according to learners' readiness to learn' (1980: 44).

  First, as Brookfield (1986) comments, these two assumptions can easily lead to a technological interpretation of learning that is highly reductionist. By this he means that things can become rather instrumental and move in the direction of competencies. Language like 'life application' categories reeks of skill-based models – where learning is reduced to a series of objectives and steps (a product orientation). We learn things that are useful rather than interesting or intriguing or because something fills us with awe. It also thoroughly underestimates just how much we learn for the pleasure it brings (see below).

  Second, as Humphries (1988) has suggested, the way he treats social roles – as worker, as mother, as friend, and so on, takes as given the legitimacy of existing social relationships. In other words, there is a deep danger of reproducing oppressive forms.

4. Orientation to learning. As a person matures, his time perspective changes from one of postponed application of knowledge to immediacy of application. With this change, orientation toward learning shifts from one of subject-centeredness to one of problem centeredness. This is not something that Knowles sees as 'natural' but rather it is conditioned (1984: 11). It follows from this that if young children were not conditioned to be subject-centred then they would be problem-centred in their approach to learning. The question here does not relate to age or maturity but to what may make for effective teaching. We also need to note here the assumption that adults have a greater wish for immediacy of application. Tennant (1988: 22) suggests that a reverse argument can be made for adults being better able to tolerate the postponed application of knowledge.

Last, Brookfield argues that the focus on competence and on 'problem-centeredness' in Assumptions 3 and 4 undervalues the large amount of learning undertaken by adults for its innate fascination. 'Much of adults' most joyful and personally meaningful learning is undertaken with no specific goal in mind. It is unrelated to life tasks and instead represents a means by which adults can define themselves' (Brookfield 1986: 99).

5. Motivation to learn. As a person matures the motivation to learn is internal (Knowles 1984: 12). Again, Knowles does not see this as something 'natural' but as conditioned – in particular, through schooling. This assumption sits awkwardly with the view that adults' readiness to learn is 'the result of the need to perform (externally imposed) social roles and that adults have a problem-centered (utilitarian) approach to learning' (Tennant 1988: 23).

In sum it could be said that these assumptions tend to focus on age and stage of development. As Ann Hanson (1996: 102) has argued, this has been at the expense of questions of purpose, or of the relationship between individual and society.

In the context of teaching in the global classroom, Table 5.1 presented by Jarvis (1985) clearly articulates the differences and therefore the implications for the educator at university level. However, when we overlay the impact of a multicultural classroom, it takes on more significance in terms of challenging some of the basic assumptions about curriculum development, interpretation, teaching style, anticipated outcomes, educational standards and how teaching occurs.

It would appear from reading widely, that all too often the basic premise of higher education is that, 'We the (teacher, the school, the discipline, the university or college), offer what we have deemed to be appropriate, in a manner that we deem to be appropriate. If a student chooses our education system, then they inherently accept our assumptions.' However, evidence is emerging that the psychological, cultural and educational principles that apply in a monocultural classroom are inadequate for effective learning in a multicultural classroom.

Table 5.1   A comparison of the assumptions of pedagogy and andragogy following Knowles

	Pedagogy	Andragogy
The learner	*Dependent.* Teacher directs what, when, how a subject is learned and tests that it has been learned	*Moves towards independence. Self-directing.* Teacher encourages and nurtures this movement
The learner's experience	*Of little worth.* Hence teaching methods are didactic	*A rich resource for learning.* Hence teaching methods include discussion, problem-solving etc.
Readiness to learn	*People learn what society expects them to.* So that the curriculum is standardized	*People learn what they need to know,* so that learning programmes organized around life application
Orientation to learning	*Acquisition of subject matter.* Curriculum organized by subjects	*Learning experiences should be based around experiences,* since people are performance-centred in their learning

Source: Jarvis (1985: 51).

From the above discourse we can identify the characteristics that underpin effective adult learning and that these do in fact differ from children's learning. As educators we need to be clear that we espouse and practice effective adult learning principles in our interactions with content, students, teaching and materials.

To return to the six assumptions underpinning pedagogical methodology and applying them to andragogical methodology we find them differing substantially in their principles and practice as described by Knowles et al. (2005):

1. The need to know. Adults need to know why they need to learn something before undertaking to learn it. The role of the facilitator is to help the learner become aware of the 'need to know'.
2. The learner's self-concept. Adults have a concept of being responsible for their own decisions, for their own lives. Once they have arrived at that self-concept, they develop a deep psychological need to be seen by others and treated by others as being capable of self-direction.
3. The role of experience. Adults come into an educational activity with both a greater volume and a different quality of experience from that

of young people. The difference in quantity and quality of experience has several consequences for adult education. It assumes heterogeneity of background, experiences, learning styles, motivation, needs, goals and aspirations. Hence the emphasis for the facilitator is on individualization of teaching and learning strategies.

4. Readiness to learn. Adults become ready to learn those things they need to know and to be able to do in order to cope effectively with their real-life situations.
5. Orientation to learning. Adults are life-centred (or task-centred or problem-centred) in their orientation to learning. Adults are motivated to learn to the extent that they perceive that learning will help them perform tasks or deal with problems that they confront in their life situations.
6. Motivation. Adults are responsive to some external motivators (better jobs, promotions, higher salaries and the like), but the most potent motivators are internal pressures (the desire for increased job satisfaction, self-esteem, quality of life and the like).

In the global business classroom with students from many different cultures and therefore differing life experiences, the implications of the above are quite dramatic. Whilst the core material to be learnt may be predetermined, the methodology of facilitating learning needs to take account of the six areas discussed above. For instance, a Norwegian classroom discussing strategy should reflect upon the orientation of the strategy content (be it Eastern or Western) and allow the student body to understand the relevance of the content to the application in the Norwegian setting (need to know). And the process of imparting knowledge and facilitating learning needs to allow for the varying experiences of the student body in terms of how they synthesize the knowledge and relate it to their real-life experience. Application of a theory of marketing can vary significantly depending on the cultural context in which it is to be applied.

What emerges here is the awareness that the andragogical model is a system of alternative sets of assumptions, a transactional model, that speaks to those characteristics of the learning situation. So that in fact, the andragogical model supplements the pedagogical model in that its application is dependant on the learning situation in which it is to be applied.

This leads to a discussion on the role of the teacher in the learning process. You may have observed how the language applied when talking of the pedagogical model utilized the term 'teacher', whereas in the andragogical model the term applied was 'facilitator'. Rogers (1969) makes the claim that in his view teaching and the imparting of knowledge make sense in an unchanging environment, which is why it has been an unquestioned function for centuries: 'But if there is one truth about modern man, it is that he lives in an environment which is continually changing.' Rogers goes on to suggest that the goal of education must be the facilitation of learning. Rogers (1969) sees the role of an educator to be that of a facilitator, and that the role is based on the personal relationship between the facilitator and the learner, which in turn is dependent on the facilitator's possessing three attitudinal qualities:

1. Realness or genuineness.
2. Non-possessive caring, prizing, trust and respect.
3. Empathic understanding and sensitive and accurate listening skills.

Knowles et al. (2005: 85–7) describe Rogers's guidelines for a facilitator of learning as follows:

- The facilitator has much to do with setting the initial mood or climate of the group or class experience. If the facilitator's own basic philosophy is one of trust in the group and in the individuals who compose the group, then this point of view will be communicated in many subtle ways.
- The facilitator helps to elicit and clarify the purposes of the individuals in the class as well as the more general purposes of the group. The facilitator can create a climate of learning by permitting individuals a sense of freedom in stating what they would like to do in their learning experience.
- The facilitator relies on the desire of each student to implement those purposes that have meaning for him or her as the motivational force behind significant learning. Even if the desire of the student is to be guided by someone else, the facilitator can accept such a need and motive and can either serve as a guide when this is desired or can provide other means, such as a set course of study, for the student whose major desire is to be dependent.
- The facilitator endeavours to organize and make easily available the widest possible range of resources for learning. Be these writings, online readings, equipment, trips, it is the goal to provide the student with the resource they may wish to use in their own enhancement and for the fulfilment of their own purposes.
- The facilitator regards himself or herself as a flexible resource to be used by the group. They do not downgrade themself as a resource. They are available as a counsellor, lecturer, advisor, person with experience.

- In responding to expressions in the classroom group, the facilitator accepts both intellectual content and the emotionalized attitudes, endeavouring to give each aspect the approximate degree of emphasis that it has for the individual or the group. Insofar as the facilitator can be genuinely doing so, he or she accepts rationalizations and intellectualizing, as well as deep and real personal feelings.
- As the acceptant classroom climate becomes established, the facilitator is increasingly able to become a participant learner, a member of the group expressing his or her views as those of one individual only.
- The facilitator takes the initiative in sharing their feelings as well as thoughts with the group – in ways that do not demand or impose but represent simply the personal sharing that students may take or leave. In this way the facilitator is free to express their own feelings in giving back feedback to students, in reacting to them as individuals, and in sharing personal satisfactions and disappointments. In such expressions it is the facilitator's 'owned' attitudes that are shared, not judgements or evaluations of others.
- Throughout the classroom experience, the facilitator remains alert to the expressions indicative of deep or strong feelings of conflict, pain, and the like, which exist primarily within the individual. Here the facilitator endeavours to understand these from the person's point of view and to communicate his or her empathic understanding. The facilitator helps to bring these into the open for constructive understanding and use by the group.
- In this functioning as a facilitator of learning, the facilitator endeavours to recognize and accept his or her own limitations. The facilitator realizes that he or she can grant freedom to students only to the extent that he or she is comfortable in giving such freedom. Understanding the inner world of students, sharing information, participating as a fellow learner, having attitudes challenged, being comfortable challenging other's attitudes, all allow for a student-centred learning experience where the facilitator creates the right environment for the student to gain the maximum possible value from the experience.

In a multicultural classroom the qualities of effective facilitation mentioned above are critical in being able to create an environment where all students can clearly identify their own unique capacity to learn effectively. Understanding issues of communication, respect, interaction, compatibility and functionality will allow for a better learning environment.

How does Roger's work manifest itself in a lecture theatre with a group of adults wanting to learn? Watson (1960–61) provided a summary of 'what is known about learning' that suggests a set of guidelines for a facilitator of learning:

1. Behaviour which is rewarded – from the learner's point of view – is more likely to recur.
2. Sheer repetition without reward is a poor way to learn.
3. Threats and punishment have variable effects upon learning, but they can and do commonly produce avoidance behaviour in which the reward is the diminution of punishment possibilities.
4. How 'ready' we are to learn something new is contingent upon the confluence of diverse – and changing – factors, some of which include:
   a. Adequate existing experience to permit the new to be learned (we can learn only in relation to what we already know); this is particularly relevant for students of different cultures.
   b. Adequate significance and relevance for the learner to engage in learning activity (we learn only what is appropriate to our purposes).
   c. freedom from discouragement, the expectation of failure, or the threats of physical, emotional or intellectual well-being.
5. Whatever is to be learned will remain unlearnable if we believe that we cannot learn it or if we perceive it as irrelevant or if the learning situation is perceived as threatening. Again this is very relevant in the global classroom.
6. Novelty (per 4 and 5 above) is generally rewarding.
7. We learn best that which we participate in selecting and planning.
8. Genuine participation (as compared with feigned participation intended to avoid punishment) intensifies motivation, flexibility, and rate of learning.
9. An autocratic atmosphere (produced by a dominating teacher who controls direction via intricate punishments) produces in learners apathetic conformity, various – and frequently devious – kinds of defiance, scapegoating (venting hostility generated by the repressive atmosphere on colleagues), or escape . . .. An autocratic atmosphere also produces increasing dependence upon the authority, with consequent obsequiousness, anxiety, shyness and acquiescence.
10. 'Closed', authoritarian environments (such as are the characteristics of most lecture theatres and classrooms) condemn most learners to continuing criticism, sarcasm, discouragement and failure, so that self-confidence, aspiration and a healthy self-concept are challenged.
11. The best time to learn anything is when whatever is to be learned is immediately useful to us.

12. An 'open' non-authoritarian atmosphere can be seen as conducive to leaner initiative and creativity, encouraging the learning attitudes of self-confidence, originality, self-reliance, enterprise and independence. All of which is equivalent to learning how to learn.

In the context of teaching in the global classroom, the deeper meaning of Rogers's and Watson's work becomes apparent when we consider students from many different nationalities. As a facilitator our level of responsibility goes beyond simply presenting material in a prescribed manner that appears to have equal meaning and relevance to all students. Each and every student has their own life experience, their own learning techniques, and their own need for the learning we are offering. Creating a 'learning environment' as a facilitator requires a greater awareness of the diversity of students and prompts the question of, 'How best can I facilitate their learning experience?' It is not, 'What have I to teach?' it is, 'What have I to learn?'

THE MOVEMENT FROM TEACHING TO LEARNING

Our discourse so far in this chapter has reflected the universal movement in higher education from the teaching paradigm to the learning paradigm. That is to say, we are now more focused on the outcomes of education – what the student learns – than on the processes and content that are utilized to induce learning. In some quarters it is seen as an either–or debate, but it is probably more realistic to see the teaching paradigm as a subset within the broader learning paradigm. By focusing on the learning paradigm we take into account the development needs of the student, their contribution to the learning process, and our capacity to facilitate a learning process that achieves desirable outcomes.

This also highlights the imperative for open consciousness of the changing classroom as we embrace students from all over the world. No matter from which country or culture we come and in which country or culture we teach, the requirements of our students can vary radically from our own, and from our own experiences of learning. For instance within the Australian higher education environment (and most other Western cultures) debate and discussion is seen as acceptable and is encouraged, so that students come prepared to express their views. Within some Asian cultures, it is inappropriate to question or to discuss with the teacher. The teacher is seen as the holder of all knowledge and the role of the student is to absorb all the teacher has to offer. How, then, does an academic in a Western context encourage and facilitate discussion when a number of students find the whole concept of discussion with a lecturer totally alien, culturally offensive and enormously difficult to comprehend?

The lecturer in a multicultural classroom is not just an expert in their subject matter, be it management, leadership, strategy, marketing, finance or the like. The lecturer is also a facilitator of learning. Certainly the learning they are facilitating is within the body of knowledge in which they have an expertise, but nonetheless the learning process is as significant in this setting as is the subject expertise.

The principles of adult learning discussed here provide an easily identifiable framework for an academic to develop their teaching skills for a classroom that consists of students from many differing cultures: that the academic is there to facilitate learning, to encourage interaction and sharing, to synthesize knowledge into practical applications, and to challenge the students to take responsibility for their own learning, enhancing the learning environment and enriching the experience for both the students and themselves.

The next part of this book provides some guidelines for approaching the various different teaching and learning strategies that are generally used.

REFERENCES

Boud, D., R. Keogh and D. Walker (1985), *Reflection: Turning Experience into Learning*, London: Kogan Page.

Brookfield, S.D. (1986), *Understanding and Facilitating Adult Learning: A Comprehensive Analysis of Principles and Effective Practice*, Milton Keynes: Open University Press.

Davenport (1993), 'Is there any way out of the andragogy mess?' in M. Thorpe, R. Edwards and A. Hanson (eds), *Culture and Processes of Adult Learning*, London: Routledge, p. 114. (First published 1987.)

Dewey, J. (1933), *How We Think*, New York: D.C. Heath.

Hanson, A. (1996), 'The search for separate theories of adult learning: does anyone really need andragogy?' in R. Edwards, A. Hanson and P. Raggatt (eds), *Boundaries of Adult Learning: Adult Learners, Education and Training Vol. 1*, London: Routledge, p. 102.

Humphries, B. (1988), 'Adult learning in social work education: towards liberation or domestication', *Critical Social Policy*, **23**: 4–21.

Jarvis, P. (1985), *The Sociology of Adult and Continuing Education*, Beckenham: Croom Helm.

Knowles, M.S. (1980), *The Modern Practice of Adult Education: from Pedagogy to Andragogy*, New York, NY: Cambridge, The Adult Education Co.

Knowles, M.S. (1984), *The Adult Learner: a Neglected Species*, 3rd edn, Houston: Gulf Pub. Co., Book Division.

Knowles, M.S., E.F. Holton and R.A. Swanson (2005), *The Adult Learner*, 6th edn, Burlington, MA: Elsevier.

Macquarie Library (1981), *The Macquarie Dictionary*, Sydney: Macquarie Publishing.

Pittenger, O.E. and C.T. Gooding (1971), *Learning Theories in Educational Practice*, New York: Wiley

Reese, H.W. and W.E. Overton (1970), 'Models of development and theories of development', in L.R. Gottlet and P.B. Baltes (eds), *Life Span Developmental Psychology*, New York: Academic Press, pp. 115–45.

Rogers, C.R. (1969), *Freedom to Learn*, Columbus, OH: Merrill.

Smith, M.K. (1996, 1999), 'Andragogy', *The Encyclopaedia of Informal Education*, http://www.infed.org/lifelonglearning/b-andra.htm.

Tennant, M. (1988, 1996), *Psychology and Adult Learning*, London: Routledge.

Watson, G. (1960–61), 'What do we know about learning?' *Teachers College Record*, 253–7.

PART II

6. Curriculum design

> As things are . . . mankind are by no means agreed about the things to be taught . . . and again about the means there is no agreement. Aristotle

INTRODUCTION

Curriculum seems to have had a long past but a short history. It has been pondered in the minds of philosophers and teachers over the centuries yet only received definition in the nineteenth century, according to *The Oxford English Dictionary*. And as with most fields of endeavour, definitions reflect differing perspectives:

- 'The totality of experience of each learner under the influence of the educational institution' (Scheffer 1960).
- 'Planned actions for instruction' (McDonald in Foshay 1970).

The concept of curriculum and the difficulty in narrowing it down to one singular concept is reflected in the work of Tanner and Tanner (1980) where they reflect the changes in perception over the twentieth century. They discuss curriculum as the 'cumulative tradition of organised knowledge', curriculum as 'modes of thought', curriculum as *'race experience'*, curriculum as *'experience'*, and curriculum as 'a technological system of production'. These discourses have led to a rich and full debate with emerging views built upon the thoughts and experiences of those that have gone before leading to a clearer sense of what it all means as we embark upon this millennium.

CURRICULUM: SOME PERSPECTIVES

Curriculum design is based on particular attitudes, values and beliefs. As a result, curriculum reflects underlying assumptions about the appropriate purposes and practices of education. Freedman (1998) tells us that curriculum design is a plan for teaching and learning in which information is organized into parts (such as lessons, units or courses) that support the educational purpose as a whole. The question this view raises, though, is who defines what the 'educational purpose' is and how it is to be perceived? Is it in the interests of the student, the institution, society or humankind in general?

McNeil (1995) describes four approaches that have been particularly influential in the past in terms of approaches to curriculum: the academic approach, the humanistic approach, the technological approach and the social reconstructionist approach. The academic approach to curriculum is the dissemination of information from the professional disciplines and the conservation and maintenance of traditional knowledge. The purpose of the humanist approach is the personal fulfilment of each individual. The technological approach focuses on systematic delivery of information to students, and the social reconstructionist approach believes that a new social order can be created through education.

In a similar vein the work of Toohey (1999) goes into far greater depth, identifying five approaches to curriculum and actually developing them in terms of key criteria such as their view of knowledge, learning, assessment, content and resource requirements. Toohey's five approaches include traditional- or discipline-based, performance- or systems-based, cognitive, personal- or experiential-based, and socially critical-based perspectives of curriculum development. The depth of Toohey's work offers the novice clear guidelines to help them determine their own approach or that of the discipline or school within which they operate. Again there are parallels to the work of McNeil.

The issue for the lecturer is to understand is that as curriculum is based on particular values, attitudes and beliefs, the need to identify these clearly in the context of the student body and the international construction of the student body, underpins the outcome of the learning experience for all concerned. An awareness of these basic thoughts allows for a more effective development and delivery of content and knowledge.

THE CONCEPT OF KNOWLEDGE: A BRIEF DISCUSSION

Underpinning this discussion about curriculum is the concept of knowledge. It is argued by Bett and Smith (1998), that the separation of knowledge and learning will become wider in the twenty-first century and that therefore knowledge will become increasingly less valuable or prized as a currency of education. Their view is that technology will make access to knowledge easier and for more people than ever before. This leads to a view that analysis and interpretation are the skills of the future. Barnett (1997) goes further in arguing that it is not that the sites of knowledge production are proliferating, but that the academics' definition of knowledge is increasingly challenged.

The movement in higher education through the latter part of the twentieth century towards practical-based learning programmes, away from the uniform classical curricula, has increased the pressure on academia to define knowledge, curricula and learning in new ways, based on student-centred learning as opposed to the imparting of wisdom and knowledge based on a pure academic approach (as per McNeil's perspectives).

The concept of student-centred learning is now seen as integral to the passing on of knowledge. As Ratcliff (1997) has warned:

> Curriculum reformers, designers and researchers need to recognise that most colleges and universities are unlikely to find one form of undergraduate curriculum that best serves the learning of all students. Only in the most homogeneous of student groupings may a single curricular approach prove productive for all learners.

The implication of this is that it is not knowledge alone that academics impart. If they are responding to student-centred principles, then the learning process integrates critical analysis, communication, synthesis and clarification. One suspects traditional academics would flinch at the thought that their knowledge-imparting processes now have to consider the practical application of that knowledge. Explaining the knowledge in terms of practical application in culturally diverse settings is not the domain of traditional academia. Being able to enter a debate where notions are challenged, concepts are required to be validated and knowledge is challenged reflects the very early Socratic approach to education in its purest form.

SOME ISSUES IN CURRICULUM DEVELOPMENT

Ratcliff (1997) raises an interesting issue about curriculum in suggesting that it needs to be adapted to the context and culture from which students originate. This appears to lack credibility within the context of some higher degree programmes now on offer to students. For instance a university in Australia offers a Masters of Business Administration programme internationally, and it is not uncommon to have 40 per cent of class numbers consisting of international students. International students choose such a programme to learn Western ways of knowledge and disciplines. They expect the curriculum to represent Western 'context and culture'. The issue this raises for the academic is the contextual framework within which to present information that enhances the students' learning process and adds to their body of knowledge in a meaningful and relevant manner. Does the curriculum design represent knowledge for knowledge's sake, or knowledge as a building block of competencies irrespective of the cultural setting?

This ties in with Joseph's (2000) perspective of understanding curriculum as culture. Our culture is the lens through which we view the world and is inculcated into us from birth as a set of values that underpin our perspective of the world in which we live. This leads to a view of curriculum as not just content, but as representing behaviours and expectations based on our sense of what is right and appropriate. Slaughter and Leslie (1997) analyse the global marketplace in relation to education by considering the concept of globalization that purports to explain why particular nations are successful in a global economy. They then link changes in the global economy to higher education by describing how education has become more centralized within national strategies for achieving a higher share of global markets. It would appear that curriculum design will gradually move away from Joseph's cultural perspective as education becomes a tool of trade for individuals on an international stage. Which again raises the issues of what is knowledge, what is its purpose, and what is it that students wish to learn? Slaughter and Leslie (1997) are implying that the curriculum of the future is going to mirror global competencies based on national strategic objectives and economic development.

The theme of knowledge for competencies flows through the work of Rickmeyer (1990) who argues that higher education has done such a good job of preparing specialized people in the past that we rarely question its suitability for a complex future. This brings us to the core of the argument about curriculum development in higher education in these times of discontinuous change. Do we go back to basics? Do we move to impose higher standards? Do we define our work in terms of economic development? Rickmeyer (1990) offers a singularly challenging framework in sharing his belief in what we should expect from our graduates:

> My own belief is that we will always require people who are well versed in details (specialisation), but that the really pressing need in the twenty first century will be for people who are also better generalists. Instead of training students to be epistemologically passive, ontologically fragmented, and methodologically isolated we must empower them to become better explorers, integrators, and collaborators. Our world is changing radically and society will be seeking more reflective practitioners – people with generic competencies, who can responsibly and effectively blend thought and action to wrestle with the issues of the day.

This leads to a situational analysis for this discourse on curriculum, knowledge and learning. It would seem that curriculum must both lead society in terms of content, as well as reflect society. Can higher education continue to focus on the traditional discipline-based approaches to the imparting of knowledge? A greater capacity to integrate disciplinary perspectives, so that students have the capacity to critique existing frameworks, will lead to a greater capacity to understand and develop new approaches to the complexities of the world in which our students live and grow. Within this is the acknowledgement of the impact of the cross-cultural context in which many business schools now operate.

WRITING A SYLLABUS

When dealing with students from many different cultures, it is imperative to consider the ramifications in terms of the design and structure of the course you offer. Too often, it is easier simply to say: 'This is how we do it here, and they come here to learn it our way!' However, this ignores the point that as an educator a key role is to educate. That is, how can I best structure my materials and teaching to allow the student to gain the maximum learning from the course?

An example highlighting a perspective that takes account of the international nature of business education occurred in an Australian university that offers some insights of note. Whilst the application here was the subject area of strategy, the implications are relevant for a range and variety of subjects.

In designing a suite of strategy courses for an MBA programme in 2003, a key consideration was the international make-up of the student body. At the time approximately 40 per cent of MBA students were international students from a diverse range and variety of cultures. From the outset, this consideration was allowed for in terms of choosing relevant texts, developing teaching materials and course content.

In terms of choosing relevant texts, it was determined that texts that had an international flavour were more appropriate than those that reflected their country of origin. So texts that gave case studies from different cultures, that used examples from different countries, that spoke of cross-cultural and global issues, were identified. In preparing teaching materials, many examples of different theories were developed from differing cultural backgrounds to ensure students understood the theory within their cultural framework. In class conversations lecturers would invite students to identify and elaborate on an example from their own country, and then a full class discussion would occur allowing all students to synthesize the information and example into their own context.

In terms of content for the study guide and therefore the course, the basic principles of strategy to be emphasized within each unit were identified and then practical examples of strategy in action were referred to, drawing on a very wide base of resource material. This would include journal articles, text references, newspaper articles and web-based material. The key point was to ensure the material written and presented was not singular in its cultural context.

A series of focus groups were initiated with immediate past international students of the existing course. The purpose was to determine whether the current teaching of strategy enhanced the capacity of international students to apply the concepts and models within their own work environments on return to their home country. The underlying premise was that Eastern philosophy significantly impacts on Eastern ways of doing business, and yet much of strategy writing is based on Western approaches to business. Could we incorporate Eastern philosophy and practice into strategy courses so that the outcomes are more understandable and relevant to an international student? One student expressed clearly the expectation of the international students. 'We come here to learn how the West does strategy, even though we find some of it not relevant to our setting. If we wanted Eastern strategy we would have studied at home.' However, when it was put to them that we could rework our material so that it took account of their frameworks, international students were very positive in their expectations.

The outcomes of these discussions fell into three categories. Firstly, the attitude of the lecturer; secondly, the language issue; and thirdly, the contextual framework.

Lecturer attitude was seen as significant in the impact it had on the teaching environment. An enthusiastic lecturer or one with a passion for the subject helped bring the subject to life for students. Lecturers who read from their PowerPoint slides, did not use contemporary examples, or who did not interact with students were felt to minimize the learning opportunity. In response to this, the teaching material prepared intentionally utilizes various teaching tools to encourage the lecturer to vary the environment for students.

A second point was the international students' attitude to a lecturer. Many cultures have a high level of respect for teachers and as a result they will not challenge or engage with them. Even to ask a question is seen to be showing disrespect for the teacher's effectiveness. Whilst this is strong in Asian cultures, other students were conscious of aspects such as addressing lecturers by their first name and the informality of some lecture room environments. The thought that they could approach a lecturer for information or clarification by email or phone was a difficult process for many students.

Language usage and comprehension was a significant issue for international students but was also raised by the other students in terms of comprehending important concepts and theories. The use of colloquial language, nuances and speed of delivery impact heavily on the students' capacity to absorb information. For international students this was an enhanced issue as English is their second or third language. In response to this, examples used reflect an international approach as opposed to using only local examples.

Contextual frameworks referred to a number of areas of concern. The first is that strategy is a subject that transcends the private sector, government sector and the not-for-profit sector. Students often felt the emphasis was on the private sector and that those working in other sectors had difficulty applying strategic principles to their work environment. International students reinforced this point by adding that the political and social environment that they would be returning to is in many cases significantly different to the Australian context, and that a more inclusive perspective was relevant. For instance, democracy in Australia allows a person to be a member of Parliament without representing mainstream views. A student from Thailand, with a single-party parliamentary democracy, becomes very confused that a member of the Australian Parliament is not a member of the government.

The second contextual concern was the use of exclusively Western examples. Both local and international students felt the course would be enhanced by the use of examples from a broad global perspective. Again, this was built into the new course mainly through the use of case studies.

The principles espoused here have application within different subject areas allowing for the obvious variations in terms of the course content such as financial subjects, corporate governance, leadership, marketing and so on.

CURRICULUM AND THE CLASSROOM

What happens in the classroom reflects the outcome of the curriculum development. There are a range of classroom techniques that can assist in ensuring the learning processes are embedded with the students, particularly focusing on the international aspect of classroom composition.

Activities

Designing interactive activities around discussion points is a standard feature of most business classrooms. However, with a cross-cultural perspective, how much consideration is given to make-up of groups, how much consideration is given to activities that reflect a global perspective, how much consideration is given to creating a conducive atmosphere for activity?

People, when asked to form into groups will tend, by nature, to gravitate towards those they know and feel comfortable with. However, the argument in attracting international students to a university is the cross-fertilization of ideas. Therefore it often requires intervention on the lecturers' part to create opportunity for cross-fertilization. A simple process can be to allocate groups. But a far more interesting approach can be to ask students to find a piece of paper and a pen and to answer five questions with a one-word answer. Questions such as:

- What is your favourite colour?
- What grade do you aspire to for this subject?
- What is one word that defines a good lecture for you?
- What is one country other than your own that you would like to live in?
- What does a culturally diverse classroom offer you?

The questions can be made up to suit the situation but should bring out some thoughts on the setting.

You then give the students ten minutes to stand up, mix and mingle, and to find students with as many similar answers as themselves. It is a simple exercise, it causes interaction and mixing, it creates conversation, it increases awareness of fellow students, and so on. It also helps students form groups.

Being Globally Inclusive

Within a business teaching environment, the use of contemporary information is prevalent and important. Identifying examples from various cultures is a relatively simple process through the use of the media or the world wide web. When discussing a particular point with a group, it enhances their understanding to be able to mention current happenings in a variety of settings, all of which relate to the theme of the discussion. This allows students from different cultures to identify the application and therefore more readily synthesize the key points the lecturer wants to impart.

Readings

In setting readings and preparation for an upcoming lecture, encourage students to identify an example from their cultural environment to bring with them. This enhances their learning experience in that they need to ensure the example they choose is relevant and applicable.

The in-class discussion with groups made up of different cultural backgrounds brings an awareness of differing business practices and the application of theory in differing contexts. This embellishes the key points for each student as they assimilate the discussion into their own potential usage.

CONCLUSION

If curriculum design is about attitudes, values and beliefs, then the lecturer in a multicultural classroom can identify the principles they wish to work with. A student-focused learning experience enhances the capacity of the student to inculcate the learning into their own environment. This allows them more adequately to synthesize the knowledge learned and to come away with a grounding based on solid learning principles. Imparting knowledge in a meaningful, and culturally relevant, manner improves the learning experience for both the student and the lecturer.

DEVELOPING CURRICULUM

There are a series of questions and considerations that emerge from this chapter that can be useful when preparing a curriculum or syllabus. They can be summarized as follows:

- What is the educational purpose of the curriculum?
- What is the focus of the curriculum – the student, the institution?
- What is the approach to the curriculum that you wish to adopt? An academic approach, a humanistic approach, a technological approach or a social reconstructivist approach?
- If, in a technological society, students can easily access knowledge, then the role of the academic is that of analysis, interpretation, a facilitator of learning. How will the curriculum reflect this?
- In a multicultural classroom, the concept of student-centred learning takes on a specific meaning. Critical analysis, practical application and synthesis all require clarification. It also implies that the curriculum of the future is going to mirror global competencies based on national strategic objectives. How does our curriculum reflect this? In other words, is our curriculum creating knowledge for competencies?

- In designing the curriculum give due consideration to the lecturer's attitude to their classroom interaction. Create a course that can come alive for the student irrespective of the lecturer's attitude.
- In designing the curriculum acknowledge differing cultural contexts. Draw on multicultural examples and materials.
- In designing the curriculum create opportunities for interactive learning through stimulating activities. Bring the learning alive for students who are not using their native tongue as well as those who are most comfortable in that environment.

REFERENCES

Barnett, R. (1997), 'Realizing the university', Inaugural Lecture, London: Institute of Education.

Bett, M. and R. Smith (1998), *Developing the Credit-Based Modular Curriculum in Higher Education*, Bristish Columbia: Palmer Press.

Foshay (1970), *Curriculum for the 70s: An Agenda for Invention*, Washington, DC: National Education Association, Center for the Study of Instruction.

Freedman, K. (1998), 'Culture in curriculum: internationalizing learning by design', in J.A. Mestenhauser and B.J. Ellingboe (eds), *Reforming the Higher Education Curriculum*, Pheonix, AZ: Oryx Press.

Joseph, P.B. (2000), 'Understanding curriculum as culture', in P.B. Joseph, S.L. Bravmann, M.A. Windschitl, E.R. Mikel and N.S. Green, *Cultures of Curriculum*, Mahwah, NJ: Lawrence Erlbaun Associates, pp. 15–27.

McNeil, J. (1995), 'Curriculum and pedagogy', in P. Tacker (ed.), *Handbook of Research on Curriculum*, New York: Macmillan, 1002, pp. 486–516.

Ratcliff, J.L. (1997), 'What is a curriculum and what should it be?' in J.G. Gaff, J.L. Ratcliff Associates (eds), *Handbook of the Undergraduate Curriculum: A Comprehensive Guide to Purposes, Structures, Practices and Change*, San Francisco, CA: Jossey-Bass, pp. 5–29.

Rickmeyer, W.J. (1990), 'Paradigms and progress', in M.E. Clark and S.A. Wawrytko (eds), *Rethinking the Curriculum*, New York: Greenwood Press.

Scheffer, L. (1960), *The Language of Education*, Chicago, IL: University of Chicago Press, pp. 11–35.

Slaughter, S. and L. Leslie (1997), 'Academic capitalism: politics, policies and the entrepreneurial university', in C. Young, 'Academic capitalism in a public workplace', *Workplace*, http://www.workplace-gsc.com/workplace2-1/young.html, accessed 29 May 2002.

Tanner, D. and L.N. Tanner (1980), *Curriculum Development: Theory into Practice*, New York: Macmillan, London: Collier Macmillan.

Toohey, S. (1999), *Designing Courses for Higher Education*, Buckingham: Open University Press.

7. Lecturing

LECTURING: WHAT IS IT?

Lecturing involves a presentation by a lecturer to a group of students, often large numbers of students. Lectures involve one-way communication – from the lecturer to groups of students that can vary in size from 20 to 2000, with the possibility of questions being raised at designated intervals.

Whilst their effectiveness is often discussed, lectures are a part of almost every tertiary course (Smith 1994). The lecture is the standard method for teaching large classes, particularly at undergraduate level.

Lectures are used to transfer information to the student in an efficient, well-structured way. They can also motivate the student to self-study (Barns and Belvin 2002). In the current climate of easy access to information through the internet and other electronic sources, value-adding is important. There is a need to reflect on whether what happens in the classroom can provide more assistance to the student than reading alone.

For learners to get the most out of the lecture process it is important that they are supported to integrate socially and academically into their programme and for the cultural capital brought by these diverse learners to be accepted and valued (Zepke and Leach 2006). The learning environment needs to be comfortable and non-threatening (Anderson and Moore 1998).

Often, the problems international students experience appear to stem from poor English language skills. It is just as likely that they are the result of students having to adapt rapidly to many factors in the new environment, of which language is only one (Ryan 2000).

WHEN DOES LECTURING WORK BEST?

Lecturing is only one of a number of teaching and learning strategies that can be used in the business classroom. Understanding the limitations of any method is important when making the choice between alternative methods. Lecturing will continue to be a significant element of the teaching and learning process because of the large numbers of students in classes. Research indicates that lecturing is weak as a method for supporting and assisting students. It is important to recognise this limitation of a method so widely used.

Lectures cannot be assumed to stimulate high-order thinking (Bligh 1972, cited in Biggs 2003). Also, what happens in lectures is unlikely to inspire or change attitudes. However, there are a number of functions that lectures, well prepared and conducted, can fulfil. These include:

- Imparting information to large numbers of people and providing an overview of the subject (Marshal and Rowland 2006). This can provide a common ground for discussion and serve as a starting point for private study.
- Drawing together the main ideas around the topic and providing information regarding the teacher's personal interpretations. This can offer a unique perspective not to be found in textbooks.
- Providing a preliminary map of difficult reading material and reviewing literature that is difficult to find.
- Adapting a topic in a way that the standard text cannot. This can include exploring the relevance to the students' particular situations, working through issues surrounding the major academic debates in the subject, or exploring in detail the areas that students are likely to find confusing.
- Directing the students to the important areas on which to concentrate before an examination.

Lecturing to a large class is not a simple process. It requires considerable thought and preparation. One of the big issues to consider when using this format is that with largely one-way communication it is difficult to know what is being learned – so finding mechanisms for feedback are important. It is also important to recognize that a good lecturer is not a crowd-pleaser who simply has advanced communication skills, but a scholar who understands the topic, the learning process and the needs of the students.

ISSUES WHEN LECTURING

There are a number of issues that need to be considered when using the lecture process and these issues take on a new significance when the student body is very culturally diverse.

Expectations of both the lecturer and the students are important and it is unlikely that expectations are shared unless explained by the lecturer. For many lecturers the lecture format is one that is so familiar it is not thought about and the assumption is often made that the students also understand the process. This may not be true. Depending on their previous education experience the students may view lectures in any number of ways. They may feel they must take down all that is said; they may feel that the lecturer's view is the 'truth', not to be questioned but to be internalized. It is not unusual for students to ask for the lecturer's perspective so that they can reflect this point of view in any assessment they do. The status of the lecturer differs greatly in different cultures and so the willingness to question or discuss what the lecturer puts forward may vary considerably, and may be considered inappropriate by students from many cultures.

Many of the students will not have English as their first language and this without doubt presents a challenge for the students and the lecturers. Students' language difficulties are often put down to inappropriate testing or lowering of standards, but learning a language is much more complex than learning many other skills. Language reflects the history, culture and assumptions of the society in which it is used, and in addition universities use discipline-specific language which is not found in standard language programmes. There may in fact be differences in meaning and assumptions behind words in different countries where the same language is spoken, such as England, the United States of America and Australia. In fact many mother tongue speakers may have difficulty with some of the discipline-specific language. You have only to pick up a book on genetics or astrophysics to appreciate that despite high levels of English language ability, it has not prepared you for the way language is used in such contexts. This raises a further range of issues.

Assumptions should not be made about the background cultural knowledge of students. An example of this was a Cambodian student who decided to take O-level English in the United Kingdom. Her spoken English was fluent and she did not anticipate any difficulties; however, on completing her comprehension test she approached me puzzled. One of the questions had not made sense to her. This question had referred to a horseshoe. She knew what a horseshoe was – it fits on a horse's hoof. However, what she did not realize was that within English culture the horseshoe is also a symbol of luck, and the question had dealt with this aspect of the word.

Pronunciation may also be an issue. Many students learn English in their home countries and may never have heard a mother tongue speaker. Also many lecturers have different accents depending on where they come from. This can make understanding very difficult because whilst the student may understand the meaning of the word when seeing it written down, they may not recognize it when spoken. Lecturers may be asked by students to identify the pages of any text they are using so that students can see in writing the words they are having difficulty understanding orally.

The use of humour should be handled with care (Beaver 2006). Culture affects what is seen to be humorous, and so does context. Humour often relies on 'inside' knowledge which may leave those who are not insiders isolated. The joke may even be taken seriously or significantly misunderstood. One lecturer when discussing different website designs described some of them as 'sexy'. The Australians in the class no doubt understood this terminology and its meaning. However, the following day an international student approached the lecturer genuinely puzzled, saying that she could not understand what the website had to do with procreation. The lecturer now uses more specific language to describe websites.

Telling stories can help illustrate a point – but they must be relevant to the topic being discussed or they can be confusing. All stories should not be from the same cultural context, otherwise they are assisting only a small proportion of the class.

Lecturing often involves sustained and unchanging low-level activity on the part of students. Simply sitting listening lowers concentration. The attention span of students under these conditions is about 15 minutes.

Lectures, because of the number of students involved, tend to a universalist view. Rules are established for managing the teaching and learning process. The opportunity for a relationship between student and lecturer is small and the rules related to submission and so on are likely to be rigid. This may seem unsympathetic to students who have a particularist view. Lecturing, probably more than any other teaching or learning method, offers a very specific level of involvement. The rules are clear, extenuating circumstances are unlikely to be looked upon favourably or even allowed, and when they are allowed they are likely to be managed through an administrative process rather than personally by the lecturer. There are often rules established by the institution for things such as poor attendance and late submission of assignments.

ADDRESSING THE ISSUES

Expectations

Being clear about your assumptions and expectations is the beginning of creating an improved teaching and learning environment. Whilst critical analysis, participation and debate may be unfamiliar processes to many students, all students will benefit from understanding what you expect of them. Each lecturer has their own approach, standards and expectations. Making this clear to the students greatly assists the learning process and reduces many of the irritations that lecturers experience with students who do not appear to understand. So here are a few things that should be made clear right at the beginning.

Provide an overall context at the start of a lecture including important background knowledge that students are expected to know so that they can make connections with previous knowledge or experience.

Be specific about the structure the lecture is going to take. Lectures can take many forms. They can address several broad areas, so ensure that the topic structure is clearly identified. They can be problem-centred, where a problem is described and potential alternative solutions are suggested. They can compare different theories or approaches. Outline the purpose of the lecture clearly so that the students know what to expect.

Indicate the essential reading you expect of students and make it clear that you expect the students to read selectively.

Create a Comfortable Learning Environment

Students learn best when they feel comfortable, are clear about what is expected of them, and feel valued and competent. Our classrooms often do not create an atmosphere where students feel safe to learn.

Explain the importance of a global perspective in business. Place emphasis on the expertise in the room: students from different countries and different industries all have something to offer. This creates an atmosphere where specific knowledge is respected and valued. International students come to Western universities to study business because they want to understand these methods, and advance their careers, not to be told that learning from a different culture implies something negative about their own homeland. Whilst this is not intentionally done, it is often implied. It is also important that domestic students understand the importance to them of the international perspective. This also then makes the material covered meaningful to the students, which is very important in engaging adult learners. Provide examples from a range of contexts to reinforce relevance to a diversity of students.

The anonymity of the student can be a problem in large lectures. This can be overcome in a number of ways which also add activity to the lecture process. One way of getting students to know each other, and to assist with the learning process, is to consolidate what is being leaned. This can be done at any stage of the lecture when a particular topic has been completed. Ask the students what they have learned, what the most important issues are and to answer these questions in pairs. The students have to articulate what they have learned to a single colleague. This is not as frightening as it might be if they were addressing the whole class. They also get to know one of their fellow students and break up the passive learning process.

To reduce further the anonymity that lectures can cause, make eye contact with students. Stand in front of the lectern, not behind it. Arrive early or leave late so that you can engage informally with students.

The business classroom can be an intimidating place, particularly for those who have not studied for sometime or who come from different educational environments and are used to using a different language for their communication. Use different visual aids to support the content as this caters for different learning styles. If you want students to make notes, give them time to do so. Invite students to use email to ask questions so that they have access to you even though they may be too shy to talk to you in class.

Language

Addressing language issues can be difficult but it helps to understand the nature of the problem. Try to imagine what it would be like if you were studying an unfamiliar subject, in an unfamiliar context, in a language you had used only infrequently in the past. The barriers to understanding and communication are enormous, but most students succeed admirably. The lecturer has a significant role in facilitating an effective communication process:

- Tell students that you understand the challenges facing the international students – this not only makes the international students feel more comfortable but it illustrates to the domestic students that a lack of fluency in the spoken language does not indicate a lack of intelligence, and that what the international students are doing requires extraordinary skill, commitment and hard work.
- Speak clearly – do not use unnecessary jargon or use colloquial language. Ensure that you can be heard.
- Find stories that help illustrate your point.
- Make notes of the topics covered available to students. Provide contextual material if necessary so that you do not have to discuss this information in the class for a minority who may not know it. Spell out acronyms and abbreviations. Provide a glossary of specialized terms.
- Provide details of where further material can be found in whatever text is being used – this helps students for whom English is not a first language follow unfamiliar language.
- Consider tape-recording the lecture and making it available through the library. Alternatively let individual students tape the lectures as this enables them to listen to it over again to ensure their understanding.

Engaging the Students

Student engagement is difficult in a large class and may not be a priority. More about engagement will be covered in following chapters but there are a couple of activities that fit well in the lecture situation. Ask for questions. Repeat the question so that the whole class understands what is being asked before answering.

Students often ask poorly framed questions. By stepping in to untangle the mess and clarify the question and answer you give confidence to students to ask questions as the risk of being made to feel foolish is reduced (Weimer 2003).

Preparation

Preparation is essential for lecturing to large classes. Many students will be affected by the lecture, and time constraints and numbers will make changing course difficult, so sound preparation greatly assists the process. Plan the academic content for each lecture and think through the management procedures – what you are going to ask students to do and how you will manage that.

Prepare materials beforehand. Glossaries can be very useful for students unfamiliar with the technical language of the subject. Notes, copies of PowerPoint slides and handouts can all be prepared beforehand and can be helpful, particularly for students for whom English is not their first language.

EXAMPLES OF GOOD PRACTICE

I hand out a short questionnaire or quiz at the end of the lecture to check if the main points were understood. I then cover areas that were not well understood in the next lecture or invite students to follow these issues up in a tutorial. (Lecturer, Oxford Brookes University, cited in Ryan 2000)

I make clear at the beginning of the semester the importance of global understanding in business education and that content must be tested against different cultural and social practices. This reduces what may appear to be 'cultural imperialism' when dealing with theoretical material that emanates from largely one cultural context. (Author, Queensland University of Technology)

I never present textbook material in lectures. I allow for question and answer time even with hundreds of students. I try to relate key concepts to current newspaper articles and television reports. (Lecturer, University of Adelaide, cited in Biggs 2003)

CHECKLIST FOR GOOD PRACTICE

Have you:

- Prepared handouts for the class?
- Clearly identified objectives for the session?
- Made a glossary of specialized terms available to students?
- Arranged a recording of the lecture?
- Thought through how you are adding value in your lecture?
- Checked that the material is current and relevant?
- Considered the cultural context of your material?
- Considered the cross-cultural issues raised by the material?
- Clarified acronyms, jargon, and so on?
- Made clear the structure and purpose of your lecture?
- Made your expectations clear?
- Prepared activities you could use in your class, such as quizzes or discussion in couples, which are possible within the constraints of the classroom?
- An awareness of your own stereotyping and its potential implications?

REFERENCES

Anderson, M. and D. Moore (1998), 'Classroom globalisation: an investigation of teaching methods to address the phenomenon of students from multiple national cultures in business school classrooms', Working Paper, Monash University, Melbourne, Faculty of Business and Economics.

Barnes, D.L. and D.R. Belvin (2002), 'An anecdotal comparison of three teaching methods used in the presentation of microeconomics', *Educational Research Quarterly*, **27**(4): 41–60.

Beaver, D. (2006), 'Warning, humour can be dangerous', *ABA Banking Journal*, **98**(10): 72.

Biggs, J. (2003), *Teaching for Quality Learning at University*, 2nd edn, Milton Keynes, UK: Society for Research into Higher Education and Open University Press.

Dalglish, C. (2006), 'The international classroom: challenges and strategies in a large business faculty', *Journal of International Learning*, **12**(8).

Marshall, L. and F. Rowland (2006), *A Guide to Learning Independently*, 4th edn, Sydney: Pearson/Longman.

Ryan, J. (2000), *A Guide to Teaching International Students*, Oxford: Oxford Centre for Staff and Learning Development.

Smith, M. (1994), *Study Secrets*, Mount Waverley: Dellesta Pty Ltd.

Weimer, M. (2003), 'Focus on learning, transform teaching', *Change*, **35**(5).

Zepke, N. and L. Leach (2006), 'Improving learner outcomes in lifelong education: formal pedagogies in non-formal learning contexts', *International Journal of Lifelong Education*, **25**(5): 507–18.

8. Encouraging participation

WHY ENCOURAGE STUDENT PARTICIPATION?

Effective class participation depends on students being actively engaged in classroom activity, supportive of each other and civil in their exchanges. Class participation is one major vehicle towards achieving quality learning (Petres 2006). Participation can involve the willingness to ask questions, to answer questions put by the teacher, and to engage in discussion activities with other members of the class.

Research (in the West) shows that learning is an active rather than a passive process.

Most people learn:

- 10 per cent of what they read.
- 20 per cent of what they hear.
- 30 per cent of what they see.
- 50 per cent of what they see and hear.
- 70 per cent of what they talk over with others.
- 80 per cent of what they use and do in real life.
- 95 per cent of what they teach someone else. (Attributed to William Glasser, cited in Biggs 2003, p. 80.)

Assuming there is validity to this summary of learning effectiveness, participation and the opportunity to talk over with others what they are learning would appear to increase the effectiveness of the learning process greatly. Participation in the classroom increases the activity the student is engaged in and extends the learning they do through seeing and hearing. Other activities such as working in groups and the use of case studies in the classroom extend the possibilities for participation and are covered in detail in following chapters.

Most teachers have a genuine interest in the learning and achievements of their students and encouraging participation is one mechanism for improving the learning potential of the classroom context. Participation as a strategy draws on what we know of effective adult learning as discussed in Chapter 5. It enables students to ask questions to identify the relevance of what is being discussed to their particular circumstances. It provides an opportunity to learn about other places, different industries and practices, and individual points of view. It provides an opportunity for knowledge and perspectives to be discussed in a range of different contexts in which the issues may arise. All of these enhance learning effectiveness (Levy 2004).

Participation can enhance the relevance of lectures. It forms the basis of many systems of learning where the lecture is followed up by tutorials where participation is expected. Participation enables the students to check the accuracy of what they have learned and discuss its relevance to their context. It also enables the tutor to assess the level of understanding of students, and direct their thoughts to contemporary issues where students from particular countries or industries may have specialized knowledge (Dallimore, Hertenstein and Platt 2006; Wentland 2004; Yamane 2006).

The tutorial, and all classroom participation, provides an opportunity for using the diversity of the student body as a learning resource. Particularly in postgraduate and MBA classrooms, students come with a vast range of contemporary business knowledge. They are often at the forefront of changes in industries and economies. They can comment on the impact of changes in the global environment from a practical perspective, providing tangible examples that can be used to discuss the significance of theory. Keeping up to date with the rapid changes in the business environment is extremely difficult, but our classrooms are filled with students who have first-hand knowledge and experience. They can provide the most contemporary issues for theory to illuminate (Dalglish 2006).

What effective participation also does is enhance the individual student's self-image as they contribute to the accumulated knowledge of the class. If learning is a process of discovering one's personal relationships with people, things and ideas, then class participation would appear to be an idea tool.

ISSUES CONCERNING PARTICIPATION

While participation appears to be a very effective learning process, research suggests that participation reduces in classes where there are significant numbers of international and, particularly, non-native English language speakers. Whilst local students appear to be willing to talk publicly, present their point of view and discuss issues, international students appear much more reluctant to do so. This being the case, classroom participation can become a process that separates rather than engages students. So why do international students generally show a reluctance to participate in the classroom?

International students may not have any experience of discussion-based approaches to teaching and learning, so this needs to be handled sensitively (Ryan 2000). Knowing that they are expected to 'participate' in the class-room discussion can cause enormous anxiety for many international students. This lack of experience can mean that they need to understand the purpose of discussion, why it will be beneficial and what exactly is expected of them.

Not speaking the language of instruction fluently can also be a barrier. Participation can be inhibited by fear of embarrassment, making a mistake, using incorrect English and the resulting loss of face. Even those who wish to participate may find that they are slow to respond while they think of the right words to use, and find that someone has made their point before them (Anderson and Moore 1998).

Students can feel that they are wasting the time of others by asking questions or expressing an opinion. They may also feel that it is arrogant to put forward their view. This does not mean that they do not have a view, rather that custom makes it difficult for them to express this view in the classroom context.

In some cultures, asking a question of the teacher would imply that the teacher has not explained well, showing a lack of respect for the teacher (Ryan 2000).

ADDRESSING THE ISSUES

These challenges are not insurmountable – and the strategies for encouraging participation make participation easier, more relevant and more effective for all students. Providing a framework for participation can make this active process more meaningful for everyone concerned. It can reduce anxiety and keep those who participate too much under control. Some of the issues that need to be addressed include the following.

Expectations

Expectations are very important, particularly for students who have had no previous experience of participation. Explain the purpose of seminars, tutorials or any situation in which students are expected to 'discuss' the information they have been provided with. What sort of participation is appropriate? Can they ask questions? Will you ask questions of them? Why are you using this approach? Many students may feel that the teacher's voice is much more important than that of another student, and therefore will not listen and learn from other students' contributions.

Explain the 'rules' and expectations. How should they ask questions? When will you ask questions? If you are going to ask direct questions of individuals in class, advise them of the topics and reading in advance so that students can prepare. Give the students time to respond. Often they have to translate the answer from their native tongue into English in their head. Explain the sort of questions you are likely to ask so they have a framework as they read and prepare.

Be clear about your assumptions and expectations at the beginning of the course as this is important to create a supportive and non-threatening learning environment. Whilst participation and debate may be familiar to some of your students, all students will benefit from understanding what you expect of them. Each lecturer has their own approach, standards and expectations. Making this clear to the students greatly assists the learning process and reduces many of the irritations that lecturers experience with students who do not appear to understand. So here are a few things that should be made clear right at the beginning.

What do you mean by participation? Is it just how much you say? What you say? Do you have to say anything? Is participation being measured, and if so, how?

Create a Comfortable Learning Environment

Students learn best when they feel comfortable, are clear on what is expected of them and feel valued and competent. Our classrooms often do not create an atmosphere where students feel safe to learn or to share their experiences or perspectives (Hadjioannou 2007).

Explain the importance of a global perspective in business. Place emphasis on the expertise in the room: students from different countries and different industries all have something to offer. This creates an atmosphere where specific knowledge is respected and valued. This enhances self-confidence, a prerequisite for participation. International students come to Western universities to study business because they want to understand these methods, and advance their careers, not to be told that learning from a different culture implies something negative about their own homeland. Whilst this is not intentionally done, it is often implied. It is also important that domestic students understand the importance to them of the international perspective. This also helps the students understand why participation is important for them and their fellow students. Create opportunities for socialization between international students and other students.

Rather than asking individuals to respond to questions directly putting stress on their language skills, ask students to write down their responses and discuss them with a partner before giving a response that is shared with the whole group. This has a number of advantages. It gives the student the time to find the right words. He or she has an opportunity to try the idea out on a peer so that the risk of appearing foolish is greatly diminished. It tends also to improve the quality of the responses given.

Use pair work to encourage confidence in the students. Pair individuals who do not share a native language, so that they have to use English. Using pairs, or small groups, can facilitate students meeting each other and benefiting directly from the diversity present. These small groups can be made up of people from different industries and different age groups as well as from different cultural backgrounds. If students are to accept the benefits, not just the challenges, of working in diversity, they need to experience it first hand.

Language

Many international students will not want to draw attention to themselves. Many experience a culture shock that they did not expect, particularly early in their programme of study. This can undermine their self-confidence und their belief in their ability to be successful in such an unfamiliar environment.

Silence and passivity are seen as virtues in many cultures and it can be difficult to overcome deeply ingrained cultural practices. International students, or any students for whom English is not their first language, when faced with stressful situations such as oral presentations or answering questions in class may feel that they are not adequately prepared to participate with dignity and without loss of face. It is important to explain the benefits attached to risking this loss of dignity – and that no one will think less of them.

Give second-language speakers time to prepare what they are going to say. This can be done by asking them to prepare the week before, or by getting them to work in pairs or small groups in class to discuss the topic and frame their views before they have to share with the class as a whole.

Do not prevent students using their native language. Particularly in the early stages of their programme, this helps them become comfortable within the new environment.

Acknowledge the challenges they are facing. Acknowledge the special knowledge and expertise they bring to the classroom. Students who feel self-confident and valued are much more likely to participate than those who feel they have little to contribute.

Preparation

Preparation is essential for encouraging effective participation. You need to know exactly what you expect and why participation is important. You also need to think of the situation in which your students find themselves. What follows are some suggestions to ensure that all students have an opportunity to participate and therefore enhance their learning:

- Include tasks that require participation by all students. Think of ways in which everyone can be active. In a large class this may mean students working in groups before individuals respond to questions. This ensures that although not everyone can address the whole class each time, everyone has been part of the discussion.
- Initially set very structured task with clear guidelines. Start with something simple and as students become more confident with discussion and asking and answering questions, the tasks can become more complex. This helps everyone.
- Encourage international students to ask questions. Talk about cultural difference – the importance of their perspective for everyone. Give positive reinforcement. Students are proud of where they come from – allow them to share this pride. Ask them about relevant examples or experiences from their culture.
- Use a range of different types of participation. Be creative. Ask questions, encourage students to ask questions, use games and quizzes. Any activity that gets students thinking about the content of what you are teaching in a meaningful way will enhance learning.
- Let students use their own words and ways of expressing themselves. Do not correct their English if what they are saying is understandable. If it is difficult to understand, ask them to rephrase it – be supportive and encouraging and encourage your other students to be the same.
- Most people need time to think if you ask them a question. If you are going to ask direct questions during class, let your students know beforehand so that they can prepare.
- Recognize that reversion to their native language is sometimes necessary or a relief mechanism to enable students to sort out their thoughts.
- Students need to be sure of what is expected of them under the rubric of 'class participation'. This is particularly important if their 'participation' is to be assessed. It must be clear what the criteria for effective participation are. Petres (2006) argues that these are quantity, quality and dependability:

- Quantity: it is desirable that all students be given the opportunity to participate by asking questions, offering examples when called for and supplying evidence of personal awareness of concepts relevant to the class discussion.
- Quality is the appropriateness of the response and participation, avoiding such behaviours as repetitive responses, monopolizing participation or behaving in such a way as to discourage others.
- Participation dependability means that both students and teachers can rely on the student to attend class regularly, be attentive, not chat with others in the class, come prepared and ensure that there is equal opportunity for all students to participate in such a way as to achieve high grades.

EXAMPLES OF GOOD PRACTICE

I have found that getting students to discuss particular issues in small groups before asking questions has greatly enhanced student willingness to participate. By being clear that my expectation is that everyone will take a turn at answering questions and explaining the view of their group, students appear very willing to participate. As time goes on this happens more freely as students gain confidence in the process. (Lecturer, Queensland University of Technology)

In my IT class one of the first questions I ask, is for students to share how domain names work in their countries. The students have individual knowledge that they can share. It shows the diversity that exists within a single discipline and demonstrates how important the different knowledge can be. This sets the scene for further participation by demonstrating how relevant this diversity of knowledge and experience can be. (Lecturer, Queensland University of Technology)

CHECKLIST FOR GOOD PRACTICE

As with any other teaching method, preparation is very important. The more you think through how you will use participation and what you hope to gain from it, the more effective your strategies will be. Effective participation means that students will ask questions in class rather than take up time afterwards. You will become aware of difficulties before they become problems. And you will learn a great deal about the reality of the international environment, as experienced by a great diversity of students.

Have you:

- Clearly identified objectives for the session?
- Created a safe and supportive atmosphere in which participation will be non-threatening?
- Made your expectations for participation clear?
- An awareness of your own stereotyping and its potential implications?
- Thought about how you can use participation to enhance student learning?
- Given the students notice if you are going to ask questions related to the content, so that they can prepare?
- Thought about how you might use pairings or small groups?
- Identified other activities that might encourage participation?

REFERENCES

Anderson, M. and D. Moore (1998), 'Classroom Globalisation: an investigation of teaching methods to address the phenomenon of students from multiple national cultures in business school classrooms', Working Paper, Monash University, Melbourne, Faculty of Business and Economics.

Biggs, J. (2003), *Teaching for Quality Learning at University*, 2nd edn, Milton Keynes: Society for Research into Higher Education and Open University Press.

Dalglish, C. (2006), 'The international classroom: challenges and strategies in a large business faculty', *Journal of International Learning*, **12**(8).

Dallimore, E.J., J.H. Hertenstein and M.B. Platt (2006), 'Non-voluntary class participation in graduate discussion courses: effects of grading and cold calling', *Journal of Management Education*, **30**(2): 354–77.

Hadjioannou, X. (2007), 'Bringing the background to the foreground: what do classroom environments that support authentic discussions look like?' *American Educational Research Journal*, **44**(2): 370–99.

Levy, L. (2004), 'Most pressing issues in higher education: drawing out the voices', *Phi Kappa Phi Forum*, **84**(4): 56–7.

Petres, K. (2006), 'An operational definition of class participation', *College Student Journal*, **40**(4): 821–3.

Ryan, J. (2000), *A Guide to Teaching International Students*, Oxford: Oxford Centre for Staff and Learning Development.

Wentland, D. (2004), 'A guide for determining which teaching methodology to utilize in economics education: trying to improve how economics information is communicated to students', *Education*, **124**(4): 640–48.

Yamane, D. (2006), 'Course preparation assignments: a strategy for creating discussion based courses', *Teaching Sociology*, **34**(3): 236–48.

Zepke, N. and L. Leach (2006), 'Improving learner outcomes in lifelong education: formal pedagogies in non-formal learning contexts', *International Journal of Lifelong Education*, **25**(5): 507–18.

9.   Working in groups

> Being forced into group work at University taught me so much about why I never
> want to work in groups again. (Anonymous student, 2003)

INTRODUCTION

The argument often used in universities is that having students learn to
work in groups reflects the real world of everyday life in business. However,
does it? Is group work and working in teams in a university environment
the same as working in teams in the workplace?

Research has long indicated that group interaction is a good way for
students to learn (Nastasi and Clemens 1991; Slavin 1991; Johnson 1998).
Barber (2003), in discussing non-English-speaking students, comments
on how teamwork is essential for understanding and emotional comfort.
She identifies how teamwork helps students avoid embarrassment and
provides an opportunity to ask questions in a conducive environment
which helps them internalize the topic and relate it to their own situation
at home.

From a historical perspective, group work in universities was seen to be
an extension of lecturing as a means of imparting knowledge. Many of the
aims of group work were to enhance the lecture process. This led to the view
that group work only existed to support the proper business of teaching,
which was the formal lecture. Stenhouse (1972) and Bligh (1986) promul-
gated the view that the purpose of group activity was to teach students to
think and to engage with their own and others' learning through the articu-
lation of views.

Group work can be seen as an 'exciting, challenging and dynamic
method open to use in a variety of forms and to serve a range of purposes
appropriate to different disciplines' (Griffiths 2003). However, the experience of students is often not as described by Griffiths. Whilst there may be
a range of factors, including cultural boundaries and experiences, lecturer
training and competence in creating effective group work learning, and
group formation techniques, the reality often seems to be that students do
not understand how to work in groups and how to achieve maximum
benefit from group work.

Who instructs the students on how to work effectively in groups? A further question can be raised as to the extent to which the lecturer clearly understands effective group work and how to instruct students to achieve optimal results.

In the context of this discussion where our focus is on teaching in the global classroom, groups are combinations of students formed together to achieve discussion, synthesis, and/or assessment within a business school environment. They may consist of students of varying ages, experiences, cultural backgrounds, levels of commonality of language and levels of expectation within the particular academic environment.

SHORT-TERM GROUP WORK

There are a number of scenarios where group work can be deemed to be an effective method for teaching and learning. Within the course of a lecture, it can be appropriate to form small groups for a brief conversation about an issue or a question that will enhance the students' grasp of the material being imparted. This can be a simple question: How would you handle this situation? Or a more complex set of scenarios where different groups tackle different issues around the same theme. For instance, in marketing you may ask some groups to give examples of 'push' marketing and other groups to give examples of 'pull' marketing. In a strategy class, you may form five groups to each discuss one of Porter's Five Forces of industry analysis factors.

This process can embed knowledge for the students, enhance their synthesis of the knowledge, and apply the knowledge to particular scenarios as though they are the decision maker. This reflects the cognitive constructivism approach that says the task of the teacher is not to pass on to students the knowledge that the teacher possesses, but to put the student in a situation where they can construct the knowledge for themselves (Gallagher and Reid 1981).

An extension of this can be to form groups and allow significant time for each group to analyse a particular issue or concept in depth. For instance in a discussion on corporate governance you may form a number of groups and ask each to discuss a particular concept, and identify examples to share back with the class.

In these 'temporary' group formations some of the more critical issues of bonding around an ongoing task and working together to achieve a common goal may not surface as it is a short-term goal-oriented group formation that does not require the more formal structure of an ongoing group work project. Therefore it can be quite appropriate simply to ask the class to form into groups of whatever number of their own volition. However, if you wish to ensure diversity you may ask them to number off and all the ones, twos, threes, and so on form a group. There are other simple techniques for this process which will be elaborated on a little later in the chapter.

In these situations diversity of opinion may surface but time constraints limit the debate and tend to focus conversation and discussion. Issues of roles, leadership, functionality, scope and purpose are limited by the short-term nature of the discussion and the time limits imposed.

LONG-TERM GROUP WORK

Forming groups to work on assessment items is a different context and introduces more complex issues and considerations for both the students and the lecturer. A point of significance is that in initiating a group work project, it is beholden on the lecturer to help students participate fully in small group situations so that the learning pay-off is fully optimized. This involves consideration of the process within the broader curriculum development for the subject as well as the course as a whole.

The human element of group work is a critical factor that needs to be recognized and acknowledged. Race (2007: 126) explains that sociological research tells us repeatedly that it is human nature not to be involved with people we do not know. We suffer from thinking that we might make a mistake, look silly or be attacked. We will however get involved with people we like. This brings us back to one of the questions in the introduction of this chapter. In a work environment we are often interacting with people over a long period of time so that we become familiar and accepting of others more readily than if we had just met them. This leads to familiarity, understanding and willingness to work together, knowing and accepting our differences. In a university setting we meet fellow students once a week in a lecture environment which does not encourage personal interaction. Students are asked to form groups usually very early in the term or semester when they have not had the opportunity to meet others and get a feel for them.

In a multicultural classroom this raises the range of issues to do with effective teaching in the global classroom: cultural norms and mores that predetermine how people relate to each other, cultural and language differences, differing levels of experience and knowledge, differing concepts of adult learning and the learning process itself, and prejudice.

The university scenario is not like a work situation, in that at work you may identify a person you would not choose to socialize with but you may well respect their work ethic, or knowledge, or skill. Therefore you may be quite comfortable working with them in a group because you realize that each of you has a contribution to make. In the university scenario the student is often forced into a group without preliminaries, and should there be a clash of personality, approach or philosophy, the student does not have the time to allocate to developing a meaningful working relationship or understanding of the other personalities in the group. Group work at university is about squeezing time in around many other time demands to work singularly on a project. This highlights the need to lower barriers quickly with would-be strangers, whilst identifying, acknowledging and respecting different viewpoints, whilst focusing on a particular context to do with learning new knowledge and information.

The following discussion on group work is designed to offer tips and ideas that can be beneficial for both the lecturer and the student. For much of the material that follows, we want to acknowledge the work of Phil Race (2007) whose repeated offerings on the learning process are a major contribution to understanding groups and teams in the university setting.

GROUP SIZE

Group size offers varying opportunities and problems that need to be considered by the lecturer before announcing to the class what they require. Pairs are limited to short-term functions, can create imbalance of contribution, but can enable a weaker student to learn from a stronger student. Threes provide an easily constructed group with a balancing effect built in for disputes. Freeloading is limited and it is functional for students to arrange to meet and work together. Fours offer opportunity for delegation and collaboration, bring out the differing strengths of students, and allow for diversity in ideas and process. Fives allow for a casting vote as well as depth of work for the same reason as fours. Freeloading potential is increased with size and this can become apparent in groups of five. Beyond five in a group, issues of coordination are increased dramatically, as is the potential for freeloaders. Consideration needs to be given to the task and the function of the group to ensure a larger group is going to achieve desirable learning outcomes.

GROUP FORMATION

Formation of groups can be handled in many differing ways. Some examples were mentioned earlier in the chapter. Some other group formation techniques may include friendship groups based on students naturally self-selecting their group. Geographical groups can take two forms. The first is their geographical positioning in the room so that it is easy for them to converse in classroom discussion. Another form in the global classroom is to consider the geographical nature of the various cultures represented in the classroom and to allow like-minded cultural groups to form. Conversely, deliberately creating intercultural interaction to allow students to draw on the diversity of their geographical background can enhance their learning and understanding.

Another group formation technique can be alphabetical (first letter in the name or last letter in the name) or age groupings depending on the make-up of the class. There are any number of random techniques for group formation such as astrological groupings, performance-based groups and skill-based groups.

The critical aspect of group formation is to take account of the task to be set, the time frame available and the purpose of using group techniques. Understanding the basic interactions of groups helps to ensure that a group process enhances the learning experience for the student as well as allowing them to perform to their potential capability.

SOME THOUGHTS TO SHARE WITH STUDENTS

Group work can help students make sense of their learning and apply it practically to various scenarios. Group work also encourages interaction and sharing of knowledge, skills and experiences, increasing the willingness of students to participate.

For full-time students, group work is easier to organize, arrange and manage. For part-time students, it is problematical. Group work adds a significant pressure point in the busy schedule of a worker attempting part-time studies. For a lecturer to be cognisant of this aspect and to encourage group interaction during breaks, within the normal class time as well as external time, can ease some of the negativity automatically attached to the concept of group work.

The role of a student in group work can vary enormously depending on the make-up of the group, the size of the group, the function of the group and the personalities within the group. Helping students to understand these variables can lead to a meaningful discussion on group work practice. Is there to be a leader? If so, what is their function: coordinate, delegate, first amongst equals, adjudicate, facilitate?

That leads to the role of group members, how a group effectively allocates tasks, and what performance indicators are used. In group work there are many followers, and understanding that followership is an art in itself and effective followership is equally as important as effective leadership can help clarify people's attitudes towards their function within a group.

A discussion on what can go wrong with group work can be enlightening and beneficial for students to assist them in becoming aware of the pitfalls and taking corrective action where necessary. Performance indicators, equally distributed work loads, punctuality, commitment to process, preparation and contribution to a meeting, disruptive behaviour such as domination and passive resistance are all issues that may need to be addressed. An open discussion on these aspects can assist students to acknowledge their behaviour and attitudes and reflect on them within the context of a group process. Having the groups in their first session openly discussing a range of these points can assist them in developing a strong and focused group.

In a global classroom, awareness of cultural issues and sensitivity towards these is imperative. An ethnocentric approach severely limits the willingness of others to contribute. Acknowledging that students from some cultures will wait until spoken to, or that learning is about the expert sharing their knowledge and not about the student sharing their experiences and views, or that some cultures encourage debate and free thinking, all are factors that students should consider in their groups. There are many different ways to achieve a goal, and the fact that one person's way might be different to another's does not mean that one is less relevant or realistic. A process-driven person has as much to contribute to a learning experience as does a results-driven person. Understanding and acknowledging these variations can lead to insights and learning beyond the subject matter of the particular course or subject.

An open discussion of possible sources of conflicts within group work is a useful exercise in creating awareness as well as tools for handling potential conflict situations. Questions can be posed, including:

- What conflicts can occur?
- How to identify the root cause of the conflict?
- How to establish ownership of the conflict and identify possible avenues for resolution?
- How to ensure conflict scenarios do not destroy a project or a process?
- How to be creative in the use of conflict to enhance the outcomes of the process or the learning through the process?

Often the open discussion around these questions will have students identifying how to handle various conflict scenarios and the roles to be played within a group, either to avoid conflict or to ensure appropriate handling of the conflict situation.

SUMMATION

Group work is a very positive learning technique in a university setting, but it needs to be managed effectively and students need to be aware of the processes that can lead to complications, to enable them to avoid the pitfalls. The message in this chapter is to plan carefully and thoughtfully for group work processes and to enlighten the students to effective group processes so that they can look to group work as a positive learning experience.

The key points of this chapter are:

- Group work is a teaching tool in its own right that can contribute uniquely to the learning experience.
- Consider the cultural construction of the class. Choose group formation processes that reflect the diversity of the student body.
- Acknowledge that it is human nature to not be involved with people we do not know. Create 'get to know you' opportunities
- Consider what group size is most effective for the task at hand.
- Identify the most appropriate basis for group formation.
- Offer students some understanding of the role and benefit of group work.
- Explain roles and functions within groups.
- Openly discuss problems with group work and positive approaches to overcome the problems.

REFERENCES

Anonymous student (2003), Participant in focus group discussion, Brisbane Graduate School of Business, Queensland University of Technology.

Barber, P.D. (2003), 'Teaching non-English speaking students', *Adult Learning*, **14**(1): 29.

Bligh, D. (ed.) (1986), *Teaching Thinking by Discussion*, Guildford, UK: SRHE and NFER Nelson.

Gallagher, J.M. and D.K. Reid (1981), *The Learning Theory of Piaget and Inhelder*, CA: Brooks/Cole Publishing.

Griffiths, S. (2003), in H. Fry, S. Ketteridge and S. Marshall, *A Handbook for Teaching and Learning in Higher Education: Enhancing Academic Practice*, London: Kogan Page.

Johnson, D.W. et al. (1998), 'Cooperative learning returns to college', *Change*, July/August: 26–36.

Nastasi, B.K. and D.H. Clements (1991), 'Research on cooperative learning: implications for practice', *School Psychology Review*, **20**(1): 14–19.

Race, P. (2007), *The Lecturer's Toolkit: A Practical Guide to Assessment, Learning and Teaching*, New York: Routledge.

Slavin, R.E. (1991), 'Synthesis of research on cooperative learning', *Educational Leadership*, **48**(5): 71–82.

Stenhouse, L. (1972), 'Teaching through small group discussion: formality, rules and authority', *Cambridge Journal of Education*, **2**(1): 18–24.

10. The case method: 'learning by doing'

In opening this chapter, the authors want to acknowledge the seminal works of Louise Mauffette-Leenders, James Erskine and Michiel Leenders (2001) in the field of case study learning and teaching.

THE CASE METHOD: WHAT IS IT?

Students learn more effectively when they are involved in the learning process (Bonwell and Eison 1991; Sivan et al. 2000). Learning can take many forms and the case method has developed a solid reputation as a meaningful contributor to the learning processes of business students. The case method is a problem-based, activity-teaching method which must be based on a 'real' and authentic situation.

It is a century ago that Harvard Business School implemented the case study method for teaching business. Over that century, the methodology, experience and practice of case study teaching has refined and built on the core principles laid down at Harvard. Cases are now taught around the world covering all nature of disciplines across both undergraduate and postgraduate education. By the mid-1990s Harvard alone had a library consisting of over 30 000 cases with 5000 of these functioning in practice as a resource for universities all over the world (Kjellen et al. 1994). There are now a number of case study clearing houses that specialize in the provision of case studies to educational institutions.

Case study learning is a fully participative model of learning and is based on the Socratic method of learning. The basic tenet of case study teaching is that the student does not learn endless lists of facts, models and theorems, but learns to question, to develop the habit of logical and correct reasoning on any subject. It strongly supports the notion of critical analysis and objective reasoning. Therefore it is not the correct answer that is being looked for, it is the process of how a person came to that answer.

A case is a description of an actual situation, commonly involving a decision, a challenge, an opportunity, a problem or an issue faced by a person or persons in an organization. The case allows you to step figuratively into the position of a particular decision maker. A case, therefore, can be a media article describing some particular event or happening, it can be a prepared document detailing a happening, or it can be created to bring out certain information and processes. The essence is that a case is field-based to allow the blending of theory and practice.

Cases enable the student to learn by doing. By placing themselves in the shoes of the decision maker, they enhance their preparation to become totally professional in their field of work.

Some of the key features and the core principles that underpin case methodology help us to understand more clearly the case method and its unique contribution to business learning. These include:

- The teacher is not a teacher per se but a facilitator of learning. They are the catalyst in the exchange between the students, and in the facilitation of the learning process.
- Case studies are based on 'real-life' situations. They should reflect the actuality of an event or set of circumstances so the student is operating in 'real time', not simply learning a theoretical framework.
- Case studies are based on decision making and problem solving. Their inherent purpose is to encourage the students to solve problems and make decisions as though they are actually involved in the situation.
- Good case studies do not encourage students to identify one right answer. The purpose behind a case study is to encourage the student to analyse the situation and to draw their own conclusion based on their learning, knowledge and experience. It is the journey to the answer that is critical, not the answer itself.
- The basis of case study learning is critical analysis. The student brings their knowledge, experience and learning to the table and it is their level of interaction with the case that facilitates effective learning. Case study learning is not a passive learning process.

To further our understanding of the case study method, Mauffett-Leenders et al. (2001) identify an inventory of skills developed by the case method.

1. Analytical skills. The case method enables students to develop qualitative and quantitative frameworks to analyse business situations, including problem identification skills, data handling skills and critical thinking skills. Students are forced to reason clearly and logically in sifting carefully through the data available. This may be an unfamiliar activity for many students, and require explanation of what is involved.

2. Decision-making skills. The case method pushes students, on the basis of their analytical work, to assess what can be done and to make decisions. Students learn to generate different alternatives, to select decision criteria, to evaluate alternatives, to choose the best alternative, and to formulate congruent action and implementation plans. This requires a level of confidence that many students may not have. They will need to be encouraged to value their expertise and perspective.
3. Application skills. Cases provide an opportunity for students to practice using the tools, techniques and theories that have been learnt.
4. Oral communication skills. The case method provides ample opportunity not only to listen to colleagues but also to express views. Thus, a whole set of speaking, listening and debating skills are developed. In this exchange of ideas and arguments, students learn to think on their feet and consider others' viewpoints as well as to defend their own positions. There are particular issues here for students for whom English is not their first language.
5. Time management skills. Under the heavy pressure of case preparation and juggling of various other responsibilities, students are forced to schedule educational activities carefully and manage time effectively.
6. Interpersonal or social skills. The case method, through small group and large group discussion, promotes learning on how to deal with peers. This learning includes conflict resolution skills and practicing the art of compromise. Because so much of future work life will involve committees, task forces, boards or project teams, learning to work effectively in a group will help a student differentiate themselves from others.
7. Creative skills. Because no two business situations are quite the same, the case method encourages looking for and finding solutions geared to the unique circumstances of each case. This method invites students to use their imagination in problem solving, as there are normally multiple solutions to each case.
8. Written communication skills. Through regular and effective note-taking, case reports and case exams, students learn the skills associated with effective writing. Emphasis on writing skills varies depending on the programme the student is enrolled on, but often takes on a high priority in business programmes as it is a key factor of success for management.

A summative comment on the case method comes from Professor Katherine Merseth of Harvard Education School when she says that right from the start the case method 'was grounded in the obligation of professional education to prepare practitioners for uncertain practice' (Merseth

1996). Given the difficulties faced by international students, the case study method, if managed carefully, would appear to have great potential to help develop the skills all business students need.

WHEN DOES THE CASE METHOD WORK BEST?

The case method is only one of a range of tools available for educating business students. However, its unique strength is its real-world application of the students' skills and knowledge. It does not replace the learning of basic concepts, theories and frameworks but enhances their impact on the learning process. In undertaking a case study, students must not only learn and understand the case, but also know what theories and concepts are relevant and what the case study brings out in relation to the course curriculum. Effective facilitating of a case study teaching forum highlights the student who has not done the requisite learning prior to the forum. It also provides an opportunity for the learning to be placed in a range of international contexts.

Case methodology contributes to a course in that it assists in bringing together the material learnt and applying it to relevant scenarios. It allows these scenarios to be located anywhere across the globe and in any industry. At an undergraduate level, the case method would be introduced into a course some weeks into the programme when it can be realistically expected that the students have grasped the basic principles and need to commence synthesizing and analysing based on those principles. In a postgraduate course, it can be assumed that case methodology could be introduced at an earlier stage as there is a presumed base of knowledge based on students' prior learning.

An argument for the case study method suggests that repetition of practice leads to good practitioners. The amount of exposure to excerpts of reality results in growing professional skills (Christensen et al. 1991).

Bloom's (1965) Taxonomy of Cognitive Learning classifies a broad range of learning outcomes into six learning objective categories.

- Knowledge. State terms, specify facts, definitions, categories, ways of doing things. (No evidence of understanding is required. The learner needs only to 'boomerang' back the information given.)
- Comprehension. Change the information to a more meaningful parallel form, paraphrase, interpret, infer, imply, extrapolate when told to do so (lowest level of understanding).
- Application. Apply understanding to solve new problems in new situations when no directions or methods of solution are specified.

- Analysis. Identify components, how they are related and arranged; distinguish fact from fiction.
- Synthesis. Produce a new combination not clearly evident before (requires originality or creativity).
- Evaluation. Form criteria, make judgements, detect fallacies, evaluate, decide.

Case method has the capacity to address all six levels of Bloom's Taxonomy. Depending on the level required by the lecturer, they can manage the case study process to the required level of learning. In other words, case method allows for addressing all levels of Bloom's Taxonomy in a planned and coherent manner.

WHAT IS EXPECTED OF THE STUDENT?

Case study learning requires a student to take an active role in their learning; to respect the ethical framework of respect, trust and openness with their peers (particularly regarding diversity and confidentiality); and to be fully committed to ongoing learning. Chapter 8 provides guidelines on encouraging participation that apply equally to case study activities.

LEARNING THROUGH CASE STUDIES

The educational challenge of a case has three major dimensions to it:

1. The analytical dimension raises the question of: 'What is the case reader's task with respect to the key decision or issue in the case?' Being able to sift through the data supplied, determine the crux of the issue, and determine potential outcomes is an analytical process based on the parameters of the case at hand. Cases can have varying degrees of difficulty in terms of the information supplied requiring varying degrees of analytical skill in determining outcomes.
2. The conceptual dimension is concerned with what theories, models and concepts are useful in understanding a particular case. In some cases, these may be identified, in others there may be readings associated with the case that indicate the relevant theories, and in other cases the reader has to draw from their body of accumulated knowledge to determine what theories are applicable.
3. The presentation dimension revolves around the question: 'What is really important and relevant information here and what is still

missing?' A case with a low degree of difficulty is short, well organized, contains all the information, offers little extraneous information and is conveyed in a single simple format. A more complex case in terms of presentation is the opposite of the above points. It is long, disorganized, is missing relevant information and includes much extraneous information, and is presented in a multiple style format.

THE CASE STUDY PROCESS

Case study learning involves three stages of interaction and activity. The first is individual preparation, which is the most important in terms of potential benefits to the student. Familiarization with the case and identifying what theoretical material is relevant is paramount to successful learning with cases. The student needs to be encouraged to come up with the right analysis, solution and implementation just as if this was a real-life situation in which they had been placed. Effective individual preparation sets the foundation for the following stages. This preparation can be facilitated if the case context is seen to be relevant. Thinking about relevance in terms of all students can be a challenge. Which cultural, geographical or political context will facilitate the most learning?

The second stage is small group discussion which is the link between individual preparation and large group discussion. There are a number of reasons why small group discussion is important:

- Teaching others: to understand a case fully a student needs to be able to discuss it fully such that others understand where they are coming from with their suggested outcomes.
- Encouraging individual preparation: small group discussion is one way of ensuring everybody prepares. Peer group pressure is quite severe in a small group when one member has not completed the work expected of them.
- Speak about every case: in a small group every member has the opportunity to express themselves, which is not always the case in a large group.
- Develop communication skills: small group participation enables students to practice listening, talking, expressing and persuasion skills that enhance their overall capacity as a communicator.
- Recognize good ideas: comparing one's ideas to another's, recognizing another's ideas are better than your own and improving ideas through interaction with others are all outcomes of small group work.

- Foster teamwork: Every work environment requires the ability to work with teams of people. This is a fundamental skill that small group work encourages and enhances.
- Build confidence: in a small group it is easier to argue a view, debate alternative views and express oneself with confidence.
- Build relationships: small group discussion can be tough and demanding, but many meaningful relationships evolve from the camaraderie that develops through open, trusting communication.

The third stage is large group discussion. This is where the total quality and quantity of the debate and discussion should emerge. It is in this forum that the depth of a case may emerge from the interactive input from all the participants following their individual and small group preparation. Whilst students may have a concern or fear about expressing themselves in a large group discussion, there are a number of reasons why individuals should be prepared to participate:

- Learn by doing: knowing that they may be called upon to make a comment sharpens individual preparation and enhances the learning process.
- Respond as requested: knowing they may be called upon to participate keeps them focused on the discussion and helps to keep thoughts ordered.
- Teach others: an individual's insights and views will be different from others in the class and each student has a responsibility to share their knowledge and experience to allow others to learn from it.
- Practice public speaking: in many workplaces we are required to speak in front of others. Large group participation develops the ability to speak in public with confidence.
- Be included: the sense of belonging and participation is enhanced as students participate in discussion and debate.
- Test ideas: the security of a classroom environment allows students to test their own ideas and thinking against that of others around them. Unwillingness to share thoughts can be seen to reflect a lack of preparation.
- Get good grades: in many case study courses, class participation is an assessable item that influences the final grades. If a student is sitting there trying to avoid involvement, their learning receptors are closed off and the depth of the learning experience will pass them by, and this will be reflected in their grades.

ENCOURAGING INDIVIDUAL PARTICIPATION

Individual preparation for a case study is critical in achieving the learning outcomes case studies offer. A lecturer can facilitate good individual preparation by sharing the following points with students.

Not knowing the industry or the business can seem daunting but the standard approach to a case study is for the student to put themselves in the position of a key player in the case study. This immersion into the role allows them to become familiar with the material within a contextual framework. This approach also ensures they 'own' the problem and do not simply play the role of spectator or observer.

In preparation for a case study the student is required to go beyond simply reading the case. They have to anticipate the problems, play out the scenarios for handling the issues and consider the implications beyond the case. In other words, they have to become involved in the case as an active participant taking a problem-solving approach to the issues. The opportunity to prepare in advance can provide international students with the confidence to participate.

Mauffett-Leenders et al. (2001) give us the short-cycle preparation process that should take no more than 15 minutes and consists of:

- Step 1 – Read the opening and the closing paragraphs.
- Step 2 – Who? What? Why? When? How?
- Step 3 – Quick look at the case exhibits.
- Step 4 – Quick review of case subtitles.
- Step 5 – Skim the case body.
- Step 6 – Read the assignment questions and reflect.

The long-cycle preparation process is composed of both a detailed reading of the case and commencing the case-solving process. The long-cycle process consists of:

- Part 1 – Read the case.
- Part 2 – Apply the case-solving process:
  - Define the issues.
  - Analyse the case data.
  - Generate alternatives.
  - Select decision criteria.
  - Analyse and evaluate alternatives.
  - Select preferred alternative.
  - Develop an action and implementation plan.

Effective preparation is essential in that the preparation for a case study has to take its place within the busy world in which students operate. Explaining this process clearly to international students will mean they are equipped to participate fully and benefit from a process with which they are probably unfamiliar.

The following tips can help students immeasurably:

- Do not read the case over and over without a road map of exactly what you are looking for.
- Read and prepare at a time in the day when your personal effectiveness is high.
- Block uninterrupted periods of time.
- Follow the principle that scheduled activities take precedence over unscheduled ones.
- Read and prepare during times when you can combine this activity with others such as eating, or riding on the bus or train.
- Set a time limit for yourself and stick to it.
- There is no need to do all the preparation all at once. Allow time for reflection.
- Draw on fellow students to discuss and reflect on the case. Different perspectives can be invaluable in identifying issues and alternative courses of action.

ENCOURAGING GROUP PARTICIPATION

The benefit of the case study is often derived from the type and nature of discussion that takes place between all students. Each student brings their own perspective to the discussion based on their cultural background, experiences, education and knowledge. The interactive process of the group enhances the learning process and encourages deeper understanding and comprehension of the principles the case study is designed to bring out.

The normal case discussion covers five phases:

1. The start.
2. The issues.
3. The analysis.
4. The alternatives.
5. The action and implementation plan.

These phases parallel the case-solving model recommended for individual preparation. This consistency helps learning.

In *Education for Judgement* (1991), Christensen et al. make an extremely important point that bears consideration:

> Teaching and learning are inseparable parts of a single continuum . . . of reciprocal giving and receiving. In discussion pedagogy students share the teaching task with the instructor and one another. All teach and all learn.

The key focus of the instructor's role is to facilitate the discussion and to provide opportunity for students to maximize their learning. This can be directive or non-directive but it is based on bringing out learning opportunities for the participants (of which the instructor is one). The key role of participants is to learn through listening, talking and reflecting. The '4Ps' of involvement are the minimum requirement that should be shared with students:

- Preparation.
- Presence.
- Promptness.
- Participation.

However to gain and contribute the most, participation must reflect a total commitment to the process. Students have to be willing to share their analysis, to subject their ideas to open debate, to take risks and to critique others' positions in a positive manner. For many, this can seem a daunting task. In some cultures, participation in an educational setting is not encouraged and is in fact deemed to be disrespectful. For some, our natural tendency is to be shy and quiet in group situations, and this raises issues of how we can participate effectively. These can be significant barriers to overcome, but students should be encouraged to bring such issues to the attention of the facilitator in order to find a comfortable path that allows them to contribute within the bounds of the case study methodology.

Effective preparation in group discussion includes using preparation notes to guide input, organizing remarks so that they add to the flow of discussion and timing remarks to offer maximum contribution to the group.

OVERCOMING PARTICIPATORY PROBLEMS FOR STUDENTS

No matter what the reason may be for why we do not enjoy participating, there are some helpful hints that a lecturer can use to assist students overcome issues. There are further suggestions in Chapter 8, 'Encouraging participation'.

- Good preparation is essential. If the student feels comfortable with the material, they will find it easier to participate.
- Encourage the student to adopt an assertive attitude that allows them to feel they have something to offer.
- Encourage them to seek support from the lecturer. Perhaps the lecturer can allow them to go first to overcome anxiety about participating.
- Encourage them to make eye contact with people they know, and not to look at the whole room. Encourage them to narrow their focus to one or two people so that they feel they are talking to friends.
- Encourage them to sit near the front of the class so that psychologically they can reduce the size of the room.
- Identify other students who are reticent to participate and link them up by them challenging each other to see who can make significant contributions each week. Make it a form of contest to help encourage them.
- Encourage them to make a point of raising their hand at least once a week to offer a contribution.
- Encourage them to seek your help and support. You are there to assist their learning.

Large group discussion is an essential part of any classroom process, but particularly so in case study learning. Developing the skill of becoming a meaningful contributor is a learnt task that takes effort and concentration. However, the benefit of learning this skill will stay with the student in all walks of life once they have completed their studies. Taking time in a supportive environment to experiment with learning to be an effective contributor will enhance their quality of enjoyment and participation throughout their life. As the facilitator of this process, the lecturer can offer much to the learning of the student beyond just subject content.

CASE PRESENTATIONS

Case presentations in class can take various forms depending on the preference of the lecturer, the size of the class, the time available and the nature of the case. In terms of effective presentations there are a number of key elements and requirements to take into account:

- Organize the presentation.
- Prepare well.
- Use memory props.
- Keep it simple.
- Use quality visual aids.
- Rehearse.
- Anticipate audience reaction.

In some cases, the lecturer may invite students to provide a critique of a presentation as a means of enhancing their awareness of what makes up a good presentation. This can be a very constructive way of helping other students to reflect on how they perform under similar circumstances. Giving feedback in these circumstances can be very useful and meaningful if a few rules are followed:

- Be constructive in giving clear, honest and objective comments. Present the good points first and do it in a descriptive manner that allows those being critiqued to clearly understand their points.
- Limit observations to a few important aspects of the presentation – do not try and cover all the minute detail.
- Distinguish between content and process observations. There is the subject matter – what we talk about, and the subject manner – how we talk about it. Distinguish between these in feedback and observations.
- Encourage vicarious learning by considering your own style and modus operandi when presenting. By reflecting on the work of others, we often can learn significantly about ourselves.

CASE REPORTS

Often students will be required to submit a case report or case notes as well as make a formal presentation. These can be used for assessment purposes or simply to gauge the degree of student preparation. Again, there are a few key elements that increase the effectiveness of a case report that should be shared with students in advance:

- Be very clear on what is required.
- Review the evaluation criteria.
- Plan the report carefully.
- Write as a manager.
- Check the work.

- Make the most of it: use the experience to practice and improve written communication skills.

CASE EXAMINATIONS

These can take various forms including a take-home exam or in-class exam, either open- or closed-book. It may be a case previously discussed in class or a new case altogether. With a case handed out ahead of time, the preparation is essentially as that for a case report. As a lecturer, here are a few tips to offer students that may also form part of the criteria by which you assess the exam:

- Try to anticipate what type of questions will be asked and what analyses could be required.
- Review cases that may have similarities to this one.
- Make detailed notes of answers to anticipated questions and organize the notes.
- If prepared well, the exam is a process of organizing your ideas and conveying them effectively.

With an exam based on a case that is handed out in the exam, the preparation is obviously different and the mindset in the exam is different:

- Manage time wisely.
- If feeling overwhelmed, determine a structured process based on the six steps of the short-cycle process discussed previously.
- Think about how to present the analysis before starting to write.

No matter what style of case exam, there are a range of suggestions that are useful for students to be aware of:

- Find out and meet the lecturer's expectations.
- Plan time according to the marks allocated for each question.
- Focus energy on the content and write points clearly and simply.
- Resist the temptation to digress and stay focused on exactly what is required.
- Support recommendations quantitatively.
- If required, make sure the student hands in all exhibits and calculations.
- Use examples of real-life situations. This helps the student show they understand the concepts and theories.
- Be consistent with arguments and assumptions.

MANAGING THE LEARNING PROCESS

Case study learning is about developing critical thinking and critical analysis skills. The benefit of case study learning is that it is based on cases from the real world and the student is asked to involve themselves as though a participant. This simulation provides hands-on learning and enhances the student's capacity to cope with and understand life as it really happens. In the work environment we are constantly confronted with dilemmas, problems and situations that require critical analysis and thinking before we can determine an appropriate outcome. Developing an understanding and a familiarity with the case study method of learning will enhance all students' capabilities in work environments.

CHECKLIST FOR GOOD PRACTICE

As educators, lecturers and teachers are concerned with the learning principles relevant to their student body. The case method is a higher-order learning tool as it challenges the student to think and learn for themselves. This does not minimize the importance of the lecturer:

- You need to consider the physical facilities and their compatibility with effective case study teaching. How can you structure the room to enable effective class involvement and participation? What adjustments need to be made to the seating arrangements to create a conducive atmosphere? Consider whether student name tags might assist person-to-person communication.
- Ensure students have sufficient time to prepare adequately for their session. Student preparation involves total familiarization with the case, as well as relevant readings to which the case applies.
- You need to be clear on what the case is meant to bring out in the student learning, and having prepared sufficiently to be able to facilitate a discussion that brings out key learning outcomes.

Erskine et al. (1998) also offer a framework for lecturer preparation for case study teaching in the form of a set of teaching note headings:

1. Case title.
2. Brief synopsis of case.
3. Immediate issues (the case decision maker's key concerns).
4. Basic issues (the lecturer's reasons for using the case in the course).
5. Teaching objectives.

6.   Suggested student assignment.
7.   Suggested additional reading/data gathering.
8.   Possible teaching aids (samples, advertising material, photos, articles, videos, CD ROMs, guest presenter).
9.   Discussion questions for use in class (for use if the discussion dies, or a change in direction is desirable).
10. Case analysis (the answers to suggested student assignments).
11. Additional points to raise (beyond student assignment questions; may include what actually happened).
12. Suggested time plan (how total class time might be divided).
13. Teaching suggestions.
14. Suggested board plan (what to record on the board as discussion evolves).
15. Case teaching plan.

This framework provides a useful checklist to ensure that there has been adequate preparation.

When the class is assembled, the case can be introduced by the lecturer either giving a brief synopsis or asking various students to share briefly with the class the key features of the case. This ensures all the students have prepared, as the lecturer invites random individuals to comment. This sets the scene for detailed class discussion in either small groups or large groups depending on the teaching plan of the lecturer. An overall framework for the case discussion would include being able to define the key issues and concerns, analyse the data, determine alternative courses of action, decide on criteria to narrow down the alternatives, select the preferred alternative and then determine a detailed action and implementation plan. Depending on the case, this structure may vary, but the essence of it is to help students focus on the process of their case discussion.

The cultural factors of a multicultural classroom become apparent in the participatory patterns of students. It is imperative to the learning process that all students participate in case discussion. The lecturer's role here is paramount.

Choosing cases that reflect the cultural background of the class can be significant. Too often it is all too easy to choose cases from the lecturer's country, as they are familiar with the story. However, the rich tapestry of global cases enriches the learning experience as well as reflecting the global nature of business today.

CONCLUSION

The case method is a highly beneficial method for teaching business students. In a multicultural classroom the case method allows for intercultural awareness of business practices through choosing cases to reflect the true nature of international business. The requirements of a lecturer in the case method are different to traditional lecturing but require equal preparation. The case study method can bring to the fore the knowledge, experience and learning of students as well as allowing for the lecturer to share relevant knowledge as the process unfolds. Careful consideration of participatory practices, through creating the right environment for interactive discussion, ensures the experience of case learning is meaningful and positive.

REFERENCES

Bloom, J.S. (1965), *The Process of Learning*, Cambridge, MA: Harvard University Press.
Bonwell, C.C. and J.A. Eison (1991), *Active Learning: Creating Excitement in the Classroom, ASHE-ERIC Higher Education report No. 1*, Washington, DC: George Washington University, School of Education and Human Development.
Christensen, C.R., D. Garvin and A. Sweet (eds) (1991), *Education for Judgement*, Boston, MA: Harvard Business School Press.
Erskine, J.A., M.R. Leenders and L.A. Mauffette-Leenders (1998), *Teaching with Cases*, Ontario: Ivey Publishing.
Kjellen, B., K. Lundberg and Y. Myrman (1994), *Casemetodik. En Handbook om att undervisa och att skriva*, Stockholm: Grundutbildningsradets skriftserie nr 14.
Mauffette-Leenders, L.A., J.A. Erskine and M.R. Leenders (2001), *Learning with Cases*, Ontario: Ivey Publishing.
Merseth, K.K. (1996), 'Cases and case methods in teacher education', in J. Sikula, T.J. Buttery and E. Guyton (eds), *Handbook of Research on Teacher Education*, 2nd edn, New York: Macmillan, pp. 75–92.
Sivan, A., R. Wong Leung, C. Woon and D. Kember (2000), 'An implementation of active learning and its effect on the quality of student learning innovations', *Education and Training International*, **37**(4): 381–9.

11. Online teaching: enhancing distance learning

Kate Whiteley*

INTRODUCTION

Distance learning has a long tradition based on the dissemination of paper-based materials. Today the interactive mediums offered by new technologies are either supporting or replacing these paper-based strategies. Online teaching is now used to provide educational opportunities to those who live in remote areas, are unable to attend class, or who prefer this method of learning. In addition online teaching is being used increasingly to support classroom teaching and offers a degree of flexibility and individual tailoring not previously possible.

Various words and terms are used to describe teaching to students through 'computer mediated communication' (Godat and Whiteley-De Graaf 2007). The terms used vary between 'online teaching', 'distance learning' and 'distance education' depending on the context in which it is discussed. Simonson et al. (2003) define online teaching as 'institution-based, formal education where the learning group is separated, and where the interactive telecommunications systems are used to connect learners, resources and instructors.'

It is acknowledged that online teaching can add to 'teaching disadvantages' for students who do not have English as their first language (ENFL) (Godat and Whiteley-De Graaf 2007; Miller et al. 2000; Selwyn and Gorard 2003). This is because students from ENFL countries often require more practical teacher–student support to understand the teaching instructions, the technological process that supports the course content. In addition learning time may be required to understand and interpret the 'Western business culture' being taught in the online classroom. Where this is concerned, reference to how previous chapters have dealt with the issue can be most useful.

* Penn State University.

Today's higher education business student is often stereotyped as being 'technologically savvy'. No matter where the student is originally from, there are online teaching and learning curriculum requirements and instructional techniques that need to be addressed to enable the student to benefit from these new technologies.

ISSUES FOR STUDENTS

Studies concerning educating students through online teaching and learning methods identify a number of pedagogical problems that continue to arise. These include:

- Student frustrations due to poor instruction design of a course and curriculum.
- Limited instructor support and direction provided face-to-face (Hughes and Lewis 2003).
- Poor skill levels with the technology.
- Inadequate English language ability.
- Difficulty understanding a Western 'business culture'.

All of these can impact on students' self-esteem, leading students to 'drop out' of online class tuition (Hughes 2007: 350). Hughes (2007) suggests many reasons why students withdraw from online classes, which are varied and complex and are dependent upon the individual. It is important not to make assumptions about these reasons but to put in place strategies that allow individual concerns to be addressed.

All students, specifically students from different cultures who do not have 'native' command of English, are prone to a sense of personal exclusion, of not belonging, and can feel they are the 'outsider' even within the context of the online classroom. Instructors need to engage more with students to enhance the student's sense of belonging. This teaching engagement can encourage students to be cooperative, and participate more fully in the online activities (Godat and Whiteley-De Graaf 2007).

Important to a student's learning capacity in an online classroom is the need to be personally motivated. Guha (2001) suggests that online teaching requires the students to have a strong level of personal motivation. It can be a challenge for lecturers to facilitate the sense of engagement that leads to personal motivation.

WHY USE ONLINE LEARNING?

Before commencing the implementation of online instructional design and the development of course content, it is necessary for the instructor to understand the advantages and disadvantages presented by online instruction (Vansickle 2003). The same rules apply for sound curriculum development as appear in Chapter 6, but with additional areas to be considered. It is vital that the instructor develops a professional and coherent course curriculum that shows explicit and comprehendible teaching instructions (Godat and Whiteley-De Graaf 2007; Landsell 2001; Meyer 2002; Rossman 1999; Schrum 2000; Vansickle 2003).

Vansickle (2003: 4) asserts that 'online courses require specific guidelines, designed interactions, revamped instructor role, and retooled evaluations along with appropriate instructional design'. For the instructor of business studies there are various pedagogical questions that relate to teaching online that are problematic. These include:

- What does online teaching present to business students that can positively support traditional, face-to-face classroom instruction?
- How does online instruction provide a better delivery of teaching through interactive 'teaching tools' for all students within a multicultural classroom than traditional classroom teaching?

It is reported that teaching online to students does provide positive learning outcomes for students and can be an effective means of teaching instruction (Brewer et al. 2001; Hoffman 2002; Meyer 2002). Hoffman (2002) argues that online teaching can be more effective because it is often compulsory for students to participate actively.

Studies of students' experiences of distance learning reveal a range of perceived benefits including: flexibility and convenience (McCall 2002; Northrup 2002); working at their own pace (McCall 2002); opportunities for teacher and student collaboration (Hoffman 2002); and control of time, the environment and the velocity of student learning (Weisenberg 1999). In addition, Meyer (2002) asserts online teaching can develop critical thinking in the student. Velayo (2001) argues that students' written skills appear to improve during the course of online instruction. Vansickle (2003: 6) states that teaching through online instruction offers 'access to more open forums of content and away from the rigid structures', and notes that 'students are to be encouraged to collaborate' with the teacher.

Students feel that they are 'learning in a comfortable and non-threatening environment'. Some students can feel intimidated by their peers or teacher, or are shy and uncomfortable interacting in a face-to-face, traditional classroom. They are often more contented with educational instructions presented online (Waterhouse 2001). In addition, the opportunity to incorporate learning flexibility within a non-threatening, online environment can impact on a student's motivation to learn. For many students the learning flexibility as to where and when they participate in class provides a feeling of 'empowerment' (Oliver 1999). It can also provide students with a more relaxed and self-controlled learning experience.

But there can be problems. Numerous studies discuss the negative impact of teaching students through online instruction. Weisenberg (1999) identifies teaching and learning issues that are problematic, including technological frustration, reliance on technological support mechanisms, and miscommunication between instructor and student. Research suggests that online learning does not have any fundamental benefit compared to other methods of learning instruction such as the traditional classroom (Clark 1994; Wells and Minor 1998).

Scholars argue online teaching does not promote one-to-one personal and close interaction between the instructor and student, and therefore does not provide the student with an overall college or university experience (Guha 2001). This is important for many international students who chose a campus and educational environment in order to associate and assimilate with domestic students and teachers to develop their overall cultural and educational experience.

KEY ISSUES FOR TEACHERS

Hoffman (2002) asserts that teaching online can make it difficult for students and teachers to create professional instructor–student relationships. Teaching through an online classroom environment does not always provide an effective means of communication, because of the lack of personal contact and the time delay between when questions are asked and when the assistance and/or response is received.

Brewer et al. (2001) assert that the role of an online instructor is to ensure that confidence and competency are key elements of implementing the curriculum. There should be sufficient interaction between teacher and student and the monitoring of a student's progress is fundamental.

To address these issues, three themes associated with online instruction are commonly identified as potentially problematic. These themes are relationships, isolation and monitoring. All intertwine and impact on the outcome of a student's educational experience whilst being taught online.

Relationships

- A lack of opportunity to encourage and build a teacher–student rapport.
- Rekkedal and Qvist-Eriksen (2003) found that approximately 10 per cent of students participating in online classes do not require teaching support. However, the remainder of students that might require assistance from the instructor often do not follow through.

Isolation

Not only does the student feel isolated, but in many instances so too does the instructor (Godat and Whiteley-De Graaf 2007). For some instructors there is a feeling of lack of control and/or power over a situation. There is often concern that they are not fulfilling their teaching obligation and meeting the needs of the students.

Monitoring

- There is minimal opportunity to supervise a student's academic performance closely.
- Students who do not actively participate in regular online class sessions, and/or are behind in submitting work for assessment, may expect the educator to make contact with them, as a part of the teacher's responsibility towards the process of monitoring their education. However, for educators the need to 'follow up' students is time-consuming and can be a discouraging exercise with a minimal success rate.

ADDRESSING THE ISSUES

Tracking System

A tracking system should be facilitated by the educator. This should provide sufficient details of the students who have 'logged on'. It is a practical way of monitoring students and provides 'an early mechanism for non-engagement' (Hughes 2007). A tracking system notifies the instructor when students are not attending, or participating.

Traditional Classroom Interaction

Arrange traditional, face-to-face classes for students to attend. Present a class at the commencement and one mid-term or mid-semester. In each class, explain the goals and objectives of the course clearly and specifically. Clarify what each section of curriculum means and incorporate and reiterate the outcomes sought. This can greatly assist in identifying the students, building a teacher–student relationship and being able more effectively to address student needs.

Teacher–Student Consultation: Online Diary

Use an online diary. Provide students with your office consultation times and include reasons and expectations for meetings. Implement an online strategy to ensure that everyone knows how to use the diary. Ask students to write their names beside times in the diary. Request that students regularly check the diary, as the instructor may request to speak to a student. Such an online diary enables the instructor to have some control over individual consultation time with students. The times can be instigated by the student or the instructor. It provides an effective method for the instructor to incorporate time with students who are less inclined to approach the teacher. It offers a proactive teaching strategy and an understated approach to monitoring students' academic progress.

Audio-Visual Interaction

Implement audio and/or visual interactive concepts as part of the online classroom activity. Throughout the teaching period, provide a range of audio and visual materials for online interaction. This encourages personal contact with the teacher and students. 'Windows of relationships' are formed between teacher and student, and student and student.

Outside–In

Incorporate learning opportunities to bring the 'real world' in to the classroom. Structure classes whereby people from business organizations are included in the online experience. Include these people from the business industry in a 'chat room' audio and/or visual web link. Bring people from the outside with their experiences into the online classroom. There may also be the opportunity of setting projects for students that require them to engage with the 'real world'. This offers a 'real-life' experience. Providing interaction with the instructor and students and outside sources improves the student learning experience.

Buddy System

Implement a 'buddy system' through an online window. Arrange for two or three students to be 'buddies'. Select a name for the interactive activity. Ensure that 'buddies' meet online and provide each other with feedback or engage in discussion pertaining to the course. Ensure students' shared online experience is recorded. You can make it a course prerequisite that each 'buddy' must meet a number of times online. This process enhances learning interaction between students. It assists with students' academic development and provides opportunities for students to discuss issues relating to the course. It can encourage the development of rapport between students from very different backgrounds and enrich the students' experience of global education.

INSTRUCTIONAL DESIGN

Another teaching and learning strategy that impacts on the outcome of a student's academic performance is the online instructional design. The instructional design should be kept simple, support the course content and be clear for all students to comprehend. It should provide interesting and informative details and directions to assist students.

When creating online teaching concepts, understanding and deciding what teaching instructions and content are compatible with the design can seem complex. The following issues need to be addressed:

- Clarity: make the technical instructions clear and comprehensive. All must be coherent and easy to understand for the student and the teacher.
- Creativity: be creative in the activities you ask students to undertake. Challenge students to take alternative routes to gain information. The technical process should invite 'fun' and 'critical thinking' learning approaches to encourage student retention. Provide strategies for interaction between instructor and students and use 'outside' sources such as other business-related websites and so on. The curriculum content being taught can be supported by using teaching and learning activities such as 'interactive games'.
- Current: maintain and update most recent newsworthy information.

Ahern and Repman (1994) assert that online tuition which includes coherent current and past messages from students will enhance a student's class participation. Therefore, incorporating discussion tools into the overall online teaching and learning strategy can be effective. Brief explanations on some discussion tools are provided.

Discussion Tools

For many online teachers the personal interaction between them and the student can be problematic. Hilts et al. (2000) assert that the development and implementation of online discussions contribute more to a student's leaning outcome than their traditional, face-to-face classroom equivalents. Online discussion tools can be useful to encourage student participation and enhance self-motivation. Tools include chat rooms, threaded discussions, bulletin boards, audio-visuals and videoconferencing

Chat Room Experience

If teaching instruction involves student discussion online through a chat room, some students can feel threatened and intimidated by other students if they have to answer online questions swiftly. This raises similar issues to those raised in the classroom situation, which have to be handled carefully. There are students who can dominate online chat rooms because they are quick typists (Schrum, 2000).

Threaded Discussion

According to Brewer et al. (2001) many students prefer to learn through 'threaded' discussion because there is no need to feel pressured to be the first to answer questions online, therefore students can work at a more relaxed, personal pace.

Audio-Visual: Positive

Shin and Chan (2004: 276) discovered during research relating to 'effects of online teaching' that there were subjective notions whereby 'audio email messages helped the distance students gain a sense of class community and feel connected to the group as a whole.'

KEY ISSUES FOR STUDENTS

There are numerous studies that examine the nuances and complexities that both English-speaking and non-English-speaking higher degree students experience while learning within a multicultural, online teaching environment (see Godat and Whiteley-De Graaf 2007). Understanding of how students cope, comprehend and experience studying through online learning practices is important. There are a number of issues that can be problematic, including: relationship-building; the interaction between student and teacher, and student and student; and students' personal expectations:

- According to Berge (2002), incorporating teacher-to-student and student-to-student interaction can form relationships which encourage and enable students, through their shared experiences and personal ideals, to evaluate, examine and analyse course information in a shared, liked community. Students can feel isolated from the teacher, with a lack of verbal and non-verbal communication.
- Students may not comprehend online instructions without face-to-face communication.
- Students may not be technically competent.
- Domestic students may become frustrated if they feel international students are slowing down the process and holding them back (that is, group discussions and activities, and so on).
- International students may feel pressure from domestic students. They can sometimes experience a sense of 'hostility'.
- Ability to read and understand business language may be limited.
- Online 'chat' rooms and/or interactive audio-visual classrooms can be intimidating.

(Godat and Whiteley-De Graaf 2007; Spector and Dela Teja 2001) identify that it is imperative for the lecturer to recognize the personal challenges that students from very diverse backgrounds encounter. The challenges that have been identified throughout this book when addressing face-to-face classroom issues become of even greater significance when the medium of teaching and learning is changed. Personal challenges and day-to-day experiences for students can be daunting.

ADDRESSING STUDENT ISSUES

Interaction between the teacher and student is imperative, no matter what teaching environment is provided. It is crucial for the student to receive feedback on their academic progress (Phipps and Merisotis 2000). However, online pedagogy has traditionally had less teacher and student interaction. For many students this is problematic. Guha (2001) asserts that it is important to keep students interested with clearly defined content and supporting tasks that make the process of online learning interesting for the student.

It is important for all students to receive constructive and professional feedback on their academic progress (Kodali 1999; Northrup 2002). However, regarding students for whom English is not their first language, this is one of the most important and relevant learning challenges for them that requires attention by their instructor. It is vital that there is ongoing 'instructor feedback' as a guide to academic progress.

CHECKLIST FOR GOOD PRACTICE

An online learning environment can make a significant positive contribution to the teaching of courses. Shin and Chan (2004: 275) emphasize the importance of teaching online as being able to 'provide distance students with rich resources for learning as well as a more flexible mode of interaction with teachers and other students, thereby enriching students' learning experiences'. Therefore, as educators of online teaching and learning in a multicultural classroom the following teaching strategies should be considered:

I   Incorporate an interactive classroom experience.
N   Notify students throughout the term of their academic progress.
S   Instigate a 'diary system'.
T   Time flexibility: acknowledge individual students' capabilities.
R   Regularly monitor students' academic progress.
U   Understand individual teaching and learning strategies required for a multicultural classroom environment – as provided elsewhere in this book.
C   Clearly articulate the 'technical delivery' of course instructions and course content. Ensure that students have the technical competence required.
T   Traditional classroom experience; provide face-to-face contact at commencement and/or mid-term if possible.
I   Implement creative online instructions to address and support course text.
O   Incorporate into the learning an 'outside' personal source: people from business, industry or other organizations.

N Nominate students for the 'buddy' system. Use the diversity available in the student body to promote learning about the international context of business.

S Specify clearly the course aims, goals and teacher expectations.

REFERENCES

Ahern, T.C. and J. Repman (1994), 'The effects of technology on online education', *Journal of Research on Computing in Education*, **26**(4): 537–46.

Berge, Z.L. (2002), 'Active, interactive and reflective e-learning', *Quarterly Review of Distance Education*, **3**(2): 181–90.

Brewer, E.W., J.O. DeJonge and V.J. Stout (2001), *Moving to Online: Making the Transition from the Traditional Instruction and Communication Strategies*, Thousand Oaks, CA: Corwin Press.

Clark, R. (1994), 'Media will never influence learning', *Journal of Educational Technology Research and Development*, **42**(2): 21–9.

Godat, M. and K. Whiteley-De Graaf (2007), 'Critical thinking: from the online environment to the multicultural classroom', in M.K. McCuddy, H. van den Bosch, W.B.J. Martz, A.V. Matveev and K.O. Morse (eds), *The Challenges of Educating People to Lead in a Challenging World*, Vol. 10, Springer: pp. 361–84.

Guha, S. (2001), 'An effective way of teaching early childhood education on-line', *Childhood Education*, **77**(4): 226–9.

Hilts, S.R., N. Coppola and M. Turoff (2000), 'Measuring the importance of collaborative learning for the effectiveness: a multi-measure, multi-method approach', *Journal of Asynchronous Learning Networks*, **4**(2), http://www.aln.org/publicatons

Hoffman, D.W. (2002), 'Internet-based distance learning in higher education', *Tech Directions*, **62**(1): 28, 5p, 2c.

Hughes, G. (2007), 'Using blended learning to increase learner support and improve retention', *Teaching in Higher Education*, **12**(3): 349–63.

Hughes, G. and L. Lewis (2003), 'Who are successful online learners? Exploring the different learner identities produced in virtual learning environments', in J. Cook and D. McConnell (eds), *Communities of Practice: Research Proceedings of the 10th Association for Learning Technology Conference*, Sheffield: University of Sheffield and Sheffield Hallam University.

Kodali, S. (1999), 'Instructional strategies used to design and deliver courses online (Computer mediated communication, distance education, online education, instructional design)', *Dissertation Abstracts International*, **60**(04): 1056.

Landsell, L. (2001), 'Distance learning environment', http://www.Itlinc.com?LTL/newsletters/jan01/oln_article.htm

McCall, D.E. (2002), 'Factors influencing participation and perseverance in online distance learning courses: a case study in continuing professional education', *Dissertation Abstracts International*, **63**(5a): 1671.

Meyer, K. (2002), *Quality in distance education: Focus on on-line learning*, Higher Education Report, **29**(4), San Francisco: Jossey-Bass.

Miller, N., H. Kennedy and L. Leung (2000), 'Tending to the tamagotchi: rhetoric and reality in the use of new technologies for distance learning', in S. Wyatt,

F. Henwood, N. Miller and P. Senker (eds), *Technology and In/equality: Questioning the Information Society*, Londòn: Routledge, pp. 129–46.

Northrup, P.T. (2002), 'Online learners' preferences for interaction', *Quarterly Review of Distance Education*, 3(2): 219–26.

Oliver, R. (1999), 'On-line teaching and learning: new roles for participants', paper presented at Internationalisation, Flexible Learning and Technology Conference, Monash University, Melbourne, 27–29 September, http://www.monash.edu.au/groups/flt/1999/online.html

Phipps, R. and J. Merisotis (2000), *Quality on the Line: Benchmarks for Success in Internet-Based Distance Education*, Washington, DC: National Education Association.

Rekkedal, T. and S. Qvist-Eriksen (2003), 'Internet based e-learning: pedagogy and support systems', in H. Fritsch (ed.), *The Role of Student Support Services in E-Learning*, ZIFF Papiere, Hagen: Fern Universität, p. 121.

Rossman, M.K. (1999), 'Successful online teaching using an asynchronous learner discussion forum', *Journal of Asynchronous Learning Networks*, 3(2): http://www.aln.org/publications

Schrum, L. (2000), 'On-line teaching and learning: essential conditions for success', in L. Lau (ed.), *Distance Learning Technologies: Issues, Trends and Opportunities*, Hershey: Idea Group, pp. 91–105.

Selwyn, N. and S. Gorard (2003), 'Reality bytes: examining the rhetoric or widening educational participation via ICT', *British Journal of Educational Technology*, 34(2): 169–81.

Shin, N. and K.Y. Chan (2004), 'Direct and indirect effects of online learning on distance education', *British Journal of Educational Technology*, 35(3): 275–88.

Simonson, M., S. Smaidino, M. Albright and S. Zvacek (2003), *Teaching and Learning at a Distance: Foundations of Distance Education*, 2nd edn, Upper Saddle River, NJ: Merrill Prentice Hall.

Spector, J.M. and I. dela Teja (2001), *Competencies for Online Teaching*, Washington, DC: Office of Educational Research and Improvement.

Vansickle, J. (2003), 'Making the transition to teaching online: strategies and methods for the first-time, online instructors', http://ericfacility.org/reprod.htm

Velayo, R. (2001), 'Asynchronous approaches to teaching psychology courses online', paper presented to the American Psychological Association, San Francisco, CA.

Waterhouse, S. (2001), 'Overview of web-based pedagogical strategies', in S. Boger (ed.), *Instructional Design*, Proceedings of Society for Information Technology and Teacher Education International Conference, Orlando, FL, 5–10 March.

Weisenberg, F. (1999), 'Teaching on-line: one instructor's evolving 'theory of practice', *Adult Basic Education*, 9(3): 149, 13.

Wells, J. and K. Minor (1998), 'Criminal justice students' attitudes toward distance learning as a function of demographics', in L. Moriarty and D. Carter (eds), *Criminal Justice Technology in the 21st Century*, Springfield, IL: Charles C. Thomas.

12. Assessment

WHAT DO WE MEAN BY ASSESSMENT?

Issues to do with assessment in the tertiary setting are complex and in a state of rapid development. Add to this the increasing diversity of the student body, with diverse expectations and learning experiences, and assessment can become an area that is not only complex but frustrating as well, for both students and teachers.

Assessment is best seen in the whole context of teaching and learning. There should be a constructive alignment between instruction, learning and assessment (Gulikers et al. 2004; Biggs 2003). For classroom assessment the purpose may be to measure knowledge, to measure skill or ability, to provide feedback to the instructor, to provide feedback to the student, or some combination of all these purposes (Duncan and Noonan 2007). It is important to reflect on whether you are using assessment to measure what has been learnt or whether it is one of the means of facilitating learning (Candela et al. 2006; Dalglish 2001).

Formative or Summative Assessment

Assessment is frequently described as either formative or summative. Formative assessment happens while learning is still occurring, while summative assessment comes at the end of learning. Assessment is part of the learning process, as student learning is largely dependent on assessment and on the students' perception of the assessment requirements. This makes it vital that whatever assessment processes are used, they are aligned with the clearly articulated objectives of the learning, and that they acknowledge and respond to diversity in the student body.

It can be argued that formative assessment has the goal of promoting and enhancing student learning. Formative assessment may be used solely to inform the teacher or it may be used as a powerful means of providing feedback to students, allowing them to alter their strategies to improve learning (Frey and Schmitt 2007). Many discussions of assessment describe the purpose of formative assessment as informing the teacher, and seldom mention providing feedback to students (ibid.). The primary benefit of formative assessment is allowing students to control and improve their own learning. This can be particularly important for students who come from different educational backgrounds and who have different experiences relating to assessment. This provides them with an opportunity to judge how well they understand the new systems and how well they are absorbing complex ideas through a foreign language. Formative assessment works best when it is treated as assessment for learning rather than assessment of learning. Learning and assessment are two sides of the same coin (Gulikers et al. 2004) – they influence each other.

Authentic Assessment

One of the topical areas of assessment currently is the discussion on authentic assessment. To be authentic the assessment task must reflect the competency that needs to be assessed. The content of the assessment reflects authentic tasks that represent real-life problems. The thinking processes that experts use to solve the problems in real life are also required by the assessment task (Gulikers et al. 2004) and are therefore an integral part of authentic assessment. Authentic assessment puts special emphasis on the realistic value of the task and context. This has become significant for faculties of business which are claiming to equip their students for the 'real-world' workplace.

Authenticity is, however, subjective, which makes student perceptions important for authentic assessment to influence learning. This is particularly significant for students from diverse backgrounds who might not understand the relevance of a topic or process – or who might argue that the topic or process is not relevant to their context.

An authentic task is a problem task that confronts students with activities that are also carried out in professional practice. The users of the assessment tasks should perceive the task as representative, relevant and meaningful. This is crucial. Students must perceive the task as relevant and see the link to a situation in the real world or working situation, if they are to regard it as a valuable transferable skill. They should also see a link between the assessment task and their own personal interests. This will differ from student to student, particularly with the diversity of backgrounds found in most business classrooms today.

Gulikers et al. (2004) identified five dimensions of authentic assessment:

- Task: What do you have to do?
- Physical context: Where do you have to do it?
- Social context: With whom do you have to do it?
- Result: What has to come out of it? What is the result of your efforts?
- Criteria: How is what you done have to be evaluated or judged?

The goal of authentic assessment is the acquisition of higher-order thinking processes and competencies rather than factual knowledge. As with all assessment measures, the important question is: Does it measure what it is supposed to measure?

Criterion-Referenced and Norm-Referenced Assessment

Much that is assessed in higher education uses a norm-referencing system. That is students are compared against each other and the spread of marks reflects comparative ability or knowledge.

Criterion-referenced assessment evaluates students against a defined set of objectives or standards, and unlike norm-referenced assessment, does not compare students to each other. Criterion-referenced assessment identifies criteria that are the characteristics of the assessment results that are valued. Standards are the level of performance expected. Setting criteria and making them explicit and transparent to the learner beforehand is important in authentic assessment because this guides learning.

Clear, well-articulated criteria can be a great help to students from diverse backgrounds as it provides a clear direction for their learning. It does not attempt to compare them with others but assesses their competence against clearly articulated criteria. Everyone is clear about what is expected of them, and can prepare to bridge the gap between where they are in their learning and where the criteria require them to be. It also allows teachers to mark against these desired criteria without being unduly effected by differences in style or complexity of language ability. Where particular communication strategies are required, the criterion referencing allows these to be made explicit.

TYPES OF ASSESSMENT AND THE ISSUES

Assessment is extremely important. Whilst as teachers we may continue the emphasis on learning and the benefits it will bring, in the short term students have to meet the requirements of the assessment tasks they are set. Their learning is likely to be driven by the need to pass. Most are aware that they will be judged by others on the grades they get, as this is a surrogate for competence. They will learn what we measure.

Many students feel disadvantaged because of their lack of background cultural knowledge or experience with particular assessment methods. When working with diverse groups there is a need for assessment criteria, whatever the assessment method, to be clear, explicit and fair.

Examinations

Written, timed examinations are a traditional means of assessing students in Western business schools. These typically have been handwritten under closed-book, invigilated conditions. No resources were available for the student to call upon. Until recently even translation dictionaries were not allowed.

As an assessment method many concerns have been raised about the efficacy of this method, particularly at postgraduate level. This type of traditional examination is seen to have a number of weaknesses. It relies on memory to ensure that students have the knowledge to answer the questions. This is not considered 'authentic'. The restricted time is not 'authentic' and provides little space for thinking or reflection. It appears to favour those who are able to remember and regurgitate data (Koslowski 2006).

Examinations now take on many forms from multiple choice questions to responding to a case study. The particular issues associated with case studies will be dealt with a little later. Now examinations can be handwritten or computer-based. There are closed-book examinations and open-book examinations where students can bring with them materials they might need to refer to. Open computer examinations have also presented a challenge as to whether students should be able to access the internet during their examination or perhaps even email for information. Once internet access is provided it is difficult to monitor usage. There are those who argue that in today's world open computer examinations are 'authentic' as this is how students will face challenges in the workplace. Open-book examinations also raise the spectre of plagiarism, which will be dealt with in greater detail when examining assignments as an assessment strategy.

Multiple-choice tests are primarily used in a summative way to differentiate between students and rank them. Computer technology has made these simpler to administer but it is important to understand their limitations. Good multiple-choice tests require a great deal of thought and are best used to assess knowledge of facts.

The use of examinations to assess student learning raise a number of issues in a culturally diverse classroom. Is the timing realistic? Can students for whom English is a second language read and understand what is required in the time available? Requiring any student to read a lengthy case study and answer questions in a restricted time is likely to lead to 'comprehension'-type answers rather than problem solving and critical analysis.

Contextual knowledge can be an issue in closed-book examinations where students from different cultural backgrounds have no access to resources to clarify their understanding of the questions.

It is important that the language used in examinations is clear and unambiguous. Whilst this is an issue for any student, it raises greater problems for students for whom English is not their first language.

Assignments and Essays

Assignments are commonly used as an assessment method to increase the authenticity of assessment and bring a connection between theory and the 'real world'. Assignments can take many forms, from theoretical essays to applying theoretical concepts to practical problems, either real or simulated. Many students from non-Western cultures may never have written an assignment or essay and may be unfamiliar with the styles required for academic writing in the West.

Cortazzi and Jin cited in Ryan (2000, p. 46) reflect:

> Some East European postgraduate students have difficulty understanding the British concept of an essay, particularly essay type answers in examinations. The reason is that, until recently, many Russian and Eastern European university examinations were oral. They involved students giving oral presentations on topics selected at random from a published list, which required extensive memorization as preparation. The British tendency to dismiss this as 'rote learning' could undermine students' confidence in what they have been trained to do (successfully) in a particular culture of learning.

Essay-writing outside of the examination context raises a range of potential problems, of which plagiarism is a frequently raised concern. It is important to remember that the Western view of what is plagiarism is not universally shared, and therefore explaining what is required is critical. Our request that students think for themselves may lead them to believe that quoting the work of others is not appreciated. They may not understand the significance of putting their thoughts in the context of demonstrated and acknowledged understanding of existing literature.

With the internet has arisen a range of sites where students can have their assignments written for them – or choose to buy one that has already been written. Making sure that the assignments set are closely tied to the objectives of the subject and are idiosyncratic in their approach is very important in reducing the usefulness of these sites. Thoughtful, meaningful assignment questions will increase the relevance of the assignment to the students and reduce the risk that they try to find an easy way to complete a pointless task.

Another important question with regard to essay and assignment topics is the relevance of the assignment to understanding the subject and to the particular context within which the student will have to use the knowledge.

Case Study

Case study analysis is a popular teaching method but it is also used extensively as an assessment tool. Case study analysis helps develop and identify a student's capacity to analysis, synthesize and problem-solve. Relevance is a key issue here. Is the relevance of the case to their learning clear to the student? Is additional cultural or historical knowledge required to understand the case fully? If this is the case, some students will be at a disadvantage.

Oral

Whilst oral examinations are no longer common, presentations are often part of the assessment processes. Fluency with language can be a key issue, particularly if the criteria for the success of the presentation are not clear. It takes considerable confidence to stand up in front of a group of peers to disclose your knowledge and understanding of a topic. Caution is required to ensure that it is the content, not the presentation skills, that are being measured – unless, of course, it is a communications course.

Applied Projects

To increase the authenticity of assessment many business programmes include projects which require students to engage with the 'real world'. They are also usually required to work in a group. Some of the special issues associated with group assessment will be considered later, but there are specific considerations where project work is concerned.

Where projects require contact with real companies in the local environment, any student who is not familiar with the local community, who has no network of local family and friends, will be at a disadvantage. Often projects require a range of local knowledge and skills that may not be universally present in students.

Group Assessment

Many students will identify that group activities are among the best and the worst of their learning experiences. Where group activities are being assessed a high level of stress is introduced into the group. Time constraints, inadequate intercultural communication skills, and underdeveloped team skills can cause group assessment to be a stressful and unrewarding process.

There is recognition that the ability to work as a participating and productive member of a group is a skill that students will require in the workplace and this has led to increased use of group assessment. It is however debatable whether group assessment leads to enhanced capacity to work as a member of a group. As mentioned before, students are driven by the assessment – so achieving results is the order of the day, not productive group work. This can leave members of the group overworked, or excluded, so as to meet the assessment criteria, leaving a feeling of unfairness or inadequacy among group members.

Working in a group is important. Listening to and understanding others is important. Sharing ideas and perspectives is important. All of this can be undertaken by using groups for discussion in class without the constraint of being assessed. In the real world people often work as part of a team but are usually assessed as individuals. There is much to be gained from using this model in the classroom. This allows risk-taking in the group. Students can stop and listen without feeling they may be penalized. Students can disagree, without feeling they are slowing down the process (King and Behnke 2005).

It seems that group assessment is important only when it is group skills that are being assessed. If one of the criteria is the nature of the group process, and the roles filled, this makes reflecting on group processes and listening to others part of what has to be achieved. Appropriate group behaviour will be assessment-driven.

For successful group assessment a number of issues need to be addressed:

- How to identify individual performance.
- What the purpose of the group activity is.
- What process you want the students to use.
- How to cope with freeloading.

ADDRESSING THE ISSUES

Many of the assessment methods described raise similar issues that need to be addressed in order to provide valid, authentic and fair assessment for all students. Here are some suggestions for addressing these issues.

Expectations

Expectations are very important. Students will be focused on learning what will be measured. So explain the method of assessment to be used, and why this particular method was chosen. Explain how the assessment works and what your expectations are. Make the criteria as clear and unambiguous as you can.

Make assessment criteria and tasks explicit and clear, and explained verbally, with examples given wherever possible. Make explicit any 'hidden agendas', for example if you deduct marks for spelling or a particular style or format.

Language

When students are operating in a language that is not their primary language of communication they are presented with a number of difficulties that arise across a range of assessment strategies. Make the language clear and unambiguous. This will help all students. Allow the use of dictionaries. In most business classrooms we are not measuring a student's vocabulary in a particular language, but their capacity to understand concepts and use them to solve problems or analyse situations. A dictionary in a foreign language will not help a student who does not understand the concept.

Be aware of context in the design of any assessment item. Make sure you are not assuming cultural knowledge that does not appear in the case or the question. Ensure that coming from a particular location would not automatically advantage or disadvantage students.

Time

Obviously students who are working in a language that is not their own will have added difficulties when they have to use this language within the time limits of a test. Be realistic about the amount of time required for reading and understanding as well as answering questions. If the examination is open-book, remember that international students will take more time to find and read the relevant texts to extract the required information (Sinclair and Wilson 1999).

One strategy that works quite well in a case study examination is to provide the case material some days before the examination. This allows students to read and reflect on the material so that they have detailed understanding of the material before they have to answer questions. This helps all students and encourages greater depth in thinking about issues than would be possible in a restricted time situation.

Plagiarism

Plagiarism is a contentious issue and one that has the potential to cause great distress to everyone concerned. Over the years of my teaching I am not convinced that deliberate plagiarism is any more common among international students than domestic students. However, what is apparent is that students for whom English is not a first language are more likely to get caught. Catching plagiarism is not the desirable outcome – preventing it is. To do this you need to:

- Discuss what is meant by plagiarism and give real examples.
- Show how to meet referencing requirements and why they are required.
- Explicitly state the consequences of not complying with rules against plagiarism.
- Make it as difficult as possible for students to copy the works of others by changing your assessment regularly and being innovative in the questions you ask and the processes you use.

All of these need to be stated orally as well as put in writing to ensure that everyone understands.

EXAMPLES OF GOOD PRACTICE

I give students simple descriptions of plagiarism and collusion:
- copying – reproducing or imitating
- collaboration – working with others
- collusion – agreement to deceive; using the words or ideas of colleagues or other students and passing them off as your own
- plagiarism – stealing someone's words or ideas and passing them off as your own.

I then give the students real examples of each of these. (Lecturer, University of Strathclyde, cited in Ryan 2000)

One of the assessment items in a core leadership unit is to develop a profile of a leader of choice. Students can choose any real leader and are encouraged to choowse someone who is relevant in some way to them. They are also allowed to use sources that are not in English as references to encourage them to look more widely for examples of leadership and to use their theoretical understanding to analyze leaders in their own context. This greatly increases the relevance of the assessment item. (Author, Queensland University of Technology)

CHECKLIST FOR GOOD PRACTICE

As with teaching, preparation of your assessment is very important. The more you think through how you will assess and what your purpose is, the more effective the assessment strategies will be. Answer these questions in preparation:

- What is the purpose of the assessment?
- Is it formative or summative?

- Is it measuring or facilitating learning?
- Is the assessment authentic?
- Are the criteria for the assessment item clear?
- Have you explained the grading system?
- Have you provide clear instructions about what the examination (or assignment) looks like (how many questions, and so on)?
- Are examination questions worded carefully and unambiguously?
- Have you used a number of different assessment formats in your course?
- Have you provide a structural framework for modelling an assignment?
- Have you allowed sufficient time for the examination, considering the amount of reading that is required?
- Can your students access dictionaries if they require them?
- Do the topics you have provided allow international students to demonstrate their knowledge or perspective?

REFERENCES

Biggs, J. (2003), *Teaching for Quality Learning at University*, 2nd edn, Milton Keynes Society for Research into Higher Education and Open University Press.

Candela, Lori, K. Dalley and J. Benzel-Lindley (2006), 'A case for learning centred curricula', *Journal of Nursing Education*, **45**(2): 59–66.

Dalglish, C. (2001), 'Using assessment to trigger transformational learning in leadership development', 8th Annual EDINEB International Conference – Technology, Pedagogy and Innovation, Nice, France, 20–22 June.

Duncan, C.R. and B. Noonan (2007), 'Factors affecting teachers' grading and assessment practices', *Alberta Journal of Educational Research*, **53**(1): 1–21.

Frey, B.B. and V.L. Schmitt (2007), 'Coming to terms with classroom assessment', *Journal of Secondary Gifted Education*, **18**(3): 402–23, 488, 491.

Gulikers, J.T.M., T.J. Bastiaens and P.A. Kirschner (2004), 'A five dimensional framework for authentic assessment', *Educational Technology, Research and Development*, **52**(3): 67–86.

King, P.E. and R.R. Behnke (2005), 'Problems associated with evaluating student performance in groups', *College Teaching*, **53**(2): 57–61.

Koslowski III, F.A. (2006), 'Quality and assessment in context: a brief review', *Quality Assurance in Education*, **14**(3): 277–88.

Ryan, J. (2000), *A Guide to Teaching International Students*, Oxford: Oxford Centre for Staff and Learning Development.

Sinclair, A. and V.B. Wilson (1999), *The Culture Inclusive Classroom*, Melbourne: Melbourne Business School, University of Melbourne.

Index